# WHAT OTHERS ARE SAYING

I loved the book! As a family medicine physician, I believe the body is all connected—it does not stop at the neck. Just as we would address and treat a thyroid condition, heart disease, or diabetes, so we also treat mental health conditions through therapy, medications, or both. Not acknowledging our mental well-being can have a pronounced effect on the rest of the body. For those who most need to hear them, James' and Faith's refreshing words are encouraging, authentic, and most of all, life-giving.

**Dr. Dawn Lagerkvist, MD**
Family Physician

Jim has done it again! From happy to hot mess, he rants, raves, and is ridiculously funny. He and his therapist daughter talk us off the ledge in this layover called life. Whether we are at our wit's end or whimsically skipping, swirling, and twirling through a field of weeping willows, this book will knock your fuzzy socks off!

**Tammy Whitehurst**
Motivational Speaker, writer,
and co-director of the Christian Communicators Conference

The father and daughter team of James and Faith Watkins provides very practical and instructive answers to many mental health issues that need our attention. Their use of healing humor and insight will change how you see yourself. Your walk with God and your mental health will never be the same.

**Dr. Tim Mills**
Licensed Clinical Psychologist

By just reading the table of contents, I knew this book was going to be good. *They get it*, I thought. *Brilliant! Funny!* Each honest, relatable, and transparent chapter cuts through the stigmas and lies with a good dose of truth plus plenty of hope and humor. The theologian and therapist team provides readers with thought-provoking, positive, and practical comfort in knowing they are not alone as they battle their unseen enemies.

**Twila Belk**
Popular conference speaker and author of *The Power to Be*

*Praise the Lord and Pass the Prozac* is an important book for those strug-gling with mental illness, their families, caregiving professionals, faith leaders, and church members. James' humor and the biblical, personal, and compassionate perspective provide hope in a space that has been dark in the church for a long time. His daughter, Faith, a licensed clinical social worker, provides professional and personal next steps in the reader's journey.

**Brenda L. Yoder**
Licensed Mental Health Counselor (LMHC)
Licensed School Counselor, and former teacher
Author of *Fledge: Launching Your Kids Without Losing Your Mind*
Co-host of the *Midlife Moms* podcast

This often-funny, yet well-researched book is based on the authors' personal experiences with mental health issues, historical heroes beset with depres-sion, and God's Word. The biblical insights and quirky tidbits of trivia from Jim and practical prescriptions for mental health from Faith will set you free to love your imperfect self and accept God's perfect love.

**Jeanette Levellie**
Author of *The Heart of Humor*, motivational speaker,
and fellow wrestler with depression

As a mental health clinician for the past twenty years, I found this book to be inspiring. For too many years individuals with mental illness have suf-fered in silence and the church has not done a great job of coming alongside those on this journey. It's time to "normalize" mental illness and understand that God has an amazing purpose for your life, and this book hit the mark. I literally could not put the book down and loved the humor and practical application. This father and daughter team shows us it's okay to not be okay and how God will use mental illness for his glory. I will definitely be using this book as a resource.

**LaSonda Sylte**
Licensed Clinical Social Worker

# PRAISE THE LORD AND PASS THE PROZAC

## A HOPEFUL, HELPFUL, HUMOROUS DEVOTIONAL

JAMES N. WATKINS
FAITH A. WATKINS, LCSW

**hope**&
**humor**
BOOKS

in coordination with EA Books Publishing, a division of Living Parables

# DEDICATION

To the brave warriors who battle unseen enemies.

# CONTENTS

# YOU WILL BE ALRIGHT

Tiffany Senabandith

*1*

Let me tell you about this aching inside
It feels like I just want to run and hide
I can't shake these feelings that are pulling me down to the ground
All I wanna do is just escape my mind
So, I grab another bottle of whatever I find
Although I'm still stuck on the bottom, I still hear that voice inside
Saying it will be alright

*Chorus*

Hold on a little bit longer,
Don't give up, you'll get stronger
You don't have to do it on your own, 'cuz you're not alone
And when the world is pulling you down
And you can't get up off the ground
Don't lose hope, the Lord is on your side
And you will be alright
You will be alright, you will be alright

*2*

I've got something to tell you
There's a light at the end of the tunnel you're going through
I know 'cuz I've been through the darkness and back
When it feels like life's just going right, then here comes another battle to fight
But there's truth to remember when you're under attack
Hang on, God can make everything alright

*Bridge*
I know the Lord is always with me
I won't be shaken for he is beside me
In times of trouble, God is my helper
I focus my eyes on the Father above
And the darkness fades away, for he keeps me alive

Listen to the song at jameswatkins.com/prozac

# INTRODUCTION

*If it seems we are crazy, \* it is to bring glory to God. And if we are in our right minds, it is for your benefit.*
2 Corinthians 5:13

## Disclaimers, legal stuff, dire warnings:

Let's begin this book with a few warnings our publisher's lawyer wants you to know:

First: I (Jim) am *not* a doctor. I don't even play one on TV.

Second: Any medical information contained herewith is intended for general educational purposes only and should not be considered a substitute for professional medical advice.

Third: For external use only. Discontinue if rash, redness, irritation, or swelling develops. If swallowed, do not induce vomiting. Side-effects may include drowsiness or mild to severe agitation. Do not read while consuming alcohol or operating heavy machinery. Keep away from open flame. Do not store above 451 degrees. Do not use near or place in water. Void where prohibited by law, taxed, or licensed.

Finally: This is *not* a self-help book on mental illness, but a devotional offering ten affirmations backed with Scripture and behavioral studies for those of us living with a variety of mental health challenges:

| | |
|---|---|
| I Am Not Alone | I Am Forgiven |
| I Am Loved | I Am Present |
| I Am Seen | I Am Empowered |
| I Am Important | I Am Victorious |
| I Am Planned | I Am Eternal |

Our friend "Zac," the anthropomorphic pill bottle, will introduce each affirmation. At the back of the book is a page with all ten affirmation which you can cut out and tape to your bathroom mirror! The ten affirmation pages also make great adult coloring pages! (Of course, this will mean you can't return the book for a refund.)

You should also know, I (still Jim) am not a mental health *expert*! I'm more of a mental health *example*! I've dealt with depression and suicidal ideation since I was a young child. I've spent hours under the covers immobilized with clinical depression. My Attention Deficit Disorder has caused me to do all kinds of harmful and humiliating things. My Obsessive-Compulsive Disorder drives me—and others—crazy. On the Myers-Briggs Type Indicator, I'm an off-the-chart introvert. And just to keep things interesting, I have a mild case of what used to be called Asperger's. It's now simply an entry ramp to the Autistic Spectrum Disorder highway. I hate having my daily rituals disrupted, I'm anxious around unfamiliar people and places, and I need twenty-four-hours' notice to be spontaneous.

So, I deal with clinical depression, serious introversion, ADD, ASD, OCD, and probably several other undiagnosed initials!

Fortunately, I am joined in this book by my daughter, Faith, who is a licensed Clinical Social Worker (LCSW), as well as a Licensed Clinical Addictions Counselor (LCAC). She has a bachelor's degree in psychology and addictions counseling as well as a master's degree in social work. She has also struggled with clinical depression and has walked through some very dark times and places.

So, I think we make a great team. I have a degree in theology and a minor in psychology, so I, the theologian, will offer you some biblical insights. Faith, the therapist, will provide behavioral strategies from her twenty years in practice. And because most of my twenty-plus traditionally-published books are filled with hope and humor, we're going to have some fun along the way. (I hope you brought snacks.)

## You are not alone

If you're dealing with any of the hundreds of issues cataloged in the

*Diagnostic and Statistical Manual of Mental Disorders*—you are indeed *not alone*. According to the World Health Organization, one in four people suffers from depression at some time in life. So, if you have three friends who have never been depressed—you probably *are*! And, you're in good company with the depressed Job, King David, and prophets Elijah and Jeremiah. Then there's the king of mood swings, Saul, as well as those with suicidal ideation: Job, King Saul, Elijah, Jonah, and Judas.

More recent examples of godly people struggling with ungodly issues: John Calvin, Martin Luther, Charles Dickens, Isaac Newton, John Wesley, Charles Spurgeon, Florence Nightingale, David Brainerd, C. S. Lewis, Martin Luther King, Jr., Joyce Meyer, Henri Nouwen, John Piper, Pope Francis, Mother Teresa, and even Christian comic Chonda Pierce.

You are in godly company with your mental health issue whether it's anxiety, PTSD, low self-esteem, any kind of addiction, eating disorder, etc. There are *forty-four million* Americans with you in the struggle! And one in twenty-five suffers from more serious issues such as schizophrenia and psychosis. So, if you think the whole world is a bit unbalanced, you're correct!

## It has little to do with your faith

Many mental illnesses are believed to be the result of chemical imbalances or traumatic events, so they most likely have *nothing* to do with your spirituality. Zip! Zero! Zilch!

They are a result of the Fall just as much as physical suffering and natural disasters. All the prayers, positive thoughts, and "good vibes" won't prevent cyclones and psychoses, dust storms and depression, or landslides and suicides.

So, to those who tell me to just have more faith, I'd love to tell them, "And you need to have more faith for your diabetes, your blood pressure, and your ED! So there!" Yeah . . . but I'm just too nice.

All of us have a cross to bear. And over the last thirty years, I have not only learned to *bear* the cross of clinical depression—and ADD, OCD, ASD, introversion, and a touch of autism—but to *embrace* it. (If you're thinking, *Jim is a few pages short of a whole book,* stick with me and I'll explain that later. And, besides, you've ripped out the last page, so again, no refund for you!)

But most of all, I want to personally assure you . . .

### There is hope—and humor

Please know that the humor in this book comes from someone who struggles as well with mental health issues. Laughter is indeed "a good medicine" and some days it's the only thing that gets me up in the morning. So, please be assured I'm laughing *with* you, not at you. And it's even okay to laugh *at* me. I'm a "fool for Christ's sake" (1 Corinthians 4:10).

Faith and I pray this devotional book will provide hope, humor, and help if you are dealing with a mental health issue or love someone who does!

So . . . Hi, I'm Jim. I have clinical depression, ADD, ASD, and OCD—and probably some other initials. But I also have hope, peace, and joy through Jesus Christ who gives me strength!

* The Greek word translated "crazy" is *exístēmi* and it can mean 1) to be amazing, astounding, or 2) to be out of one's mind, besides one's self, insane. I'll take the first definition, please. Let's have an amazing time together!

# I

# I AM NOT ALONE

*Just as our bodies have many parts and each part has a special function, so it is with Christ's body. We are many parts of one body, and we all belong to each other.*

Romans 12:4–5

# 1

# "HI, I'M DAVID. I'M BIPOLAR"

*The temptations in your life are no different*
*from what others experience.*
1 Corinthians 10:13

"Welcome to the Yom Shayne* meeting of the Shalom Support Group in Old Jerusalem for those struggling with various mental health issues," Jacob, the group's chairperson announced.

"You can probably tell someone very important is here tonight with all the men in black robes and sunglasses talking into their sleeves. Yes, we are pleased to have his majesty King David with us tonight. We would be honored, your highness, if you began our time of sharing.

"Hi, I'm David. I'm bipolar."

"Hi, David," the group in a circle responded. Although he was wearing a gold crown and royal robes with his security detail watching the door and those in attendance, no one was intimidated or shocked that the king of Israel was dealing with mental health issues.

"If you read some of my psalms, you'll see I've been going through a rough patch with bipolar. For instance, if you read Psalm 21, you see I'm having sort of a manic episode."

David pulled out a scroll. "How the king rejoices in your strength, O LORD! He shouts with joy because you give him victory" (2:1).

"I felt like I could do anything. God was with me, and I was definitely enjoying 'victory.' But then things went south in the very next psalm: 'My

God, my God, why have you abandoned me? Why are you so far away when I groan for help? Every day I call to you, my God, but you do not answer. Every night I lift my voice, but I find no relief'" (22:1–2).

"But then immediately following that psalm is my popular Twenty-Third Psalm: 'The Lord is my shepherd; I have all that I need. He lets me rest in green meadows; he leads me beside peaceful streams. He renews my strength'" (21:1–3). Each member nodded with understanding and empathy.

Another member raised his hand.

"Hi, I'm Moses.** I struggle with suicidal ideation, so I totally understand that. One day when the Israelites were on my last nerve whining about wanting meat to eat, I cried out to *I AM*. 'I can't carry all these people all by myself! The load is far too heavy! If this is how you intend to treat me, just go ahead and kill me. Do me a favor and spare me this misery!'" (Numbers 11:14).

The leader acknowledged another raised hand.

"Hi, I'm Job. I too suffer from suicidal thoughts. I remember telling God, 'Why wasn't I born dead? Why didn't I die as I came from the womb? Had I died at birth, I would now be at peace. I would be asleep and at rest'" (Job 3:11).

The man everyone knew as the weeping prophet spoke up.

"Hi, I'm Jeremiah. I felt the same way. Everyone remembers me from my writing about God having plans 'for good and not for disaster, to give us a future and a hope' (Jeremiah 29:11). But there was a time before that I wrote, 'Oh, that I had died in my mother's womb, that her body had been my grave! Why was I ever born? My entire life has been filled with trouble, sorrow, and shame'" (Jeremiah 20:18).

"Thanks to everyone for sharing. Most people at Sabbath services aren't willing to share so honestly. It's important to remember we've all had feelings of despair and despondency, but every one of you are working through those feelings and holding on to that promise of a hope and future. I'm proud of each of you."

As you read this book, I pray that you will realize you are *not* alone. I mentioned earlier biblical characters as well as Christians through the centuries have suffered greatly from mental health issues. There's even a saint of mental health: St. Dymphna! This seventh-century teenager was beheaded by her psychotic father when she refused to marry him after his wife's death.

Still not convinced you're not alone? You're a hard sell, but keep reading.

According to the National Alliance on Mental Health in 2020, one in five adults in the United States has experienced mental health issues. One in twenty-five experience serious mental disorders.

Sixty-three million Americans have anxiety disorders. One-fourth of the population experience depression some time in life. Thirteen million are diagnosed with a dual diagnosis. Ten million have bipolar disorder. And three million deal with either borderline personality, obsessive-compulsive disorder, or schizophrenia. That's a total of sixty-six million Americans.

Worldwide, the Institute for Health Metrics and Evaluation reported in 2017, that 792 million people, or more than one in ten people on planet Earth live with a mental health disorder.

Included in those staggering numbers are your authors. So, Faith and I invite you to journey with us as we share biblical stories and behavioral studies to bring hope, humor, and help. And remember, "The temptations in your life are no different from what others experience" (1 Corinthians 10:13).

You are not alone!


* Monday or "second day" on the Hebrew calendar. This won't be on the test, but you can amaze and amuse your friends with these bits of trivia throughout the book.


** Yeah, I have a degree in theology, so I do know Moses and David—and many of the rest of the group—were not contemporaries. This is pure imagination as to what a support group of biblical characters might look like. While the Shalom Support Group is totally made up, everything else in the book is backed up with biblical and behavioral scholarship and vetted by numerous mental health care professionals. I wouldn't kid about that!

## PRESCRIPTION

Hi, I'm Faith. As a therapist, I have spent countless hours in groups much like this one. Well, maybe not *exactly* like this one, but I know and believe in the healing power of the group.

In a group session, we quickly discover that we are not alone. We are surrounded by others who are going through similar struggles and probably have a lot of the same thoughts and feelings we do. Group members get it and they get you.

In a group, we may see our problems in a different light by hearing someone else's experience. It is here that we learn more about ourselves and the human experience. Having accountability in a group is a motivation to help us change and grow. As we share our goals with others, they will be able to check in with us and our progress. Groups are also confidential and anonymous, giving us a place to freely share our thoughts and feelings in a safe, private setting.

Not feeling alone and being part of a group is so healing. When I began my own journey of recovery after a painful divorce and the aftermath of looking for love in all the wrong places, I found my own biblical heroine support group of sorts. Included in my Love Addicts Anonymous (LAA) group were Rahab, the woman caught in adultery, the woman at the well, as well as others who tragically took their love lives into their own hands. In my dark hours, these women shared their experiences with me and revealed how God came near to them in their mental and emotional anguish. (I write about this at www.recoveringlove.com.)

The Bible is jam-packed with heroes and heroines of the faith who faced similar struggles as you. You can compile your own biblical support group as well. You'll be comforted to find that you are not alone.

☐ **Google "Bible characters with mental health issues"**
You'll find over thirty-five million results. (There are not thirty-five million biblical examples—just that many posts on the subject.)

☐ **Learn as much as you can about your biblical group members**
Note how they experienced their mental and emotional struggles and how God came near to them in their brokenness.

☐ **Explore in-person support groups in your area**
If you are looking for biblically-based support groups, I would suggest researching the following: Divorce Care (www.divorcecare.org), Grief Share (www.griefshare.org), and Celebrate Recovery (www.celebrate recovery.com).

☐ **Know that you are in good company and hold tight to that promise of hope and a future**

# 2

# AND I THOUGHT
# I HAD ISSUES

*The Lord is close to the brokenhearted;*
*he rescues those whose spirits are crushed.*
Psalm 34:18

Okay, we've established that many of our heroes of the Bible dealt with serious mental health issues. And many other godly believers have also struggled. Here are three intense examples:

## David Brainerd (1718–1747)

This renowned missionary to Native Americans wrote of his struggles in what Jonathan Edwards compiled as *The Life and Diary of David Brainerd.*

> I was so overwhelmed with dejection that I knew not how to live: I longed for death exceedingly: My soul was "sunk in deep waters," and "the floods" were ready to "drown me": I was so much oppressed that my soul was in a kind of horror."
>
> Was scarce ever more confounded with a sense of my own unfruitfulness and unfitness of my work, than now. Oh, what a dead, heartless, barren, unprofitable wretch did I now see myself to be! My spirits were so low, and my bodily strength so wasted, that I could do nothing at all.

### Charles Spurgeon (1834–1892)

This "Prince of Preachers" from England spoke to over ten million people by often preaching ten times a week during the 1800s. Many of his books are still in print today.

One Sunday morning he shocked his congregation of five thousand by confessing, "I am the subject of depressions of spirit so fearful that I hope none of you ever gets to such extremes of wretchedness as I go to." He later described his depression in his *Lectures to My Students* as a "seething caldron of despair" and "the bolt fastens the door of hope and holds our spirits in gloomy prison."

"This depression comes over me whenever the Lord is preparing a larger blessing for my ministry. The cloud is black before it breaks and overshadows before it yields its deluge of mercy."

### Mother Teresa (1910-1997)

After the death of this Catholic nun, who dedicated her life to ministering to the poorest of the poor and the sickest of the sick, a priest collected her writings in *Come Be My Light: The Private Writings of the Saint of Calcutta.* *

In it, she vulnerably writes of what Saint John of the Cross vividly described as "The Dark Night of the Soul." (You can read excerpts from St. John of the Cross in my book *Intimacy with Christ.*)

> In my soul I feel just that terrible pain of loss—of God not wanting me—of God not being God—of God not really existing.
>
> In the darkness . . . Lord, my God, who am I that You should forsake me?
>
> The one You have thrown away as unwanted—unloved. I call, I cling, I want—and there is no One to answer—no One on Whom I can cling; no, No One. Alone. The darkness is so dark—and I am alone.
>
> [Depression] surrounds me on all sides—I can't lift my soul to God—no light or inspiration enters my soul.

. . . Heaven, what emptiness—not a single thought of Heaven enters my mind—for there is no hope. . . . The place of God in my soul is blank—There is no God in me. Yikes! Let's stop right there, as I'm getting depressed just typing these journal entries. But it *is* comforting to know that some of God's most faithful servants suffered from fearful mental health issues.

So, we are all in this together: The apostle Paul writes:

> The temptations in your life are no different from what others experience. And God is faithful. He will not allow the temptation to be more than you can stand. When you are tempted, he will show you a way out so that you can endure (1 Corinthians 10:13).

And it's helpful to remember that this "Rejoice in the Lord always" author, also was very honest in sharing his struggles:

> We now have this light shining in our hearts, but we ourselves are like fragile clay jars containing this great treasure. This makes it clear that our great power is from God, not from ourselves.
>
> We are pressed on every side by troubles, but we are not crushed. We are perplexed, but not driven to despair. We are hunted down, but never abandoned by God. We get knocked down, but we are not destroyed. Through suffering, our bodies continue to share in the death of Jesus so that the life of Jesus may also be seen in our bodies (2 Corinthians 4:7–10).

What great news: God uses crackpots! And even though our mental health issues may make us feel "pressed," "perplexed," and "knocked down," we are "not crushed," "driven to despair" or "destroyed." And best of all, we are "never abandoned by God."

* Mother Teresa had instructed her fellow sisters to burn all her journals at her death, but obviously they didn't. If you believe in purgatory, some of her followers will no doubt be spending some extra time there.

## PRESCRIPTION

In addition to their feelings of depression and despair, David Brainerd, Charles Spurgeon, and Mother Teresa have something else in common. They all wrote out their thoughts and feelings.

Journaling is one of the best ways I have found to reduce my anxiety, slow my obsessive thoughts and ruminating, bring awareness and clarity to a situation, and regulate my emotions.

I was encouraging a client to start journaling just last week. She looked overwhelmed with the idea and asked, "What do I even write about?" Start by writing sentences or a list of things you are thankful for. Gratitude is good for your mental health. Or write about an event that was stressful or emotional.

Please be assured that journaling isn't about writing perfectly crafted, grammatically correct sentences. Be creative and let go of those preconceived ideas and myths about journaling. Write lists, create poetry, compose a song, write a letter, draw a picture, or try bulleted ournaling.

You might do it in a special notebook, on your computer, or even on Post-It notes. Perhaps you might prefer to journal in the notes app on your phone, in a text with no recipient, or speak it in a voice memo.

☐ **Express your thoughts, emotions, and desires in a safe, private place**
No matter how, on what, or where, start journaling today!

# 3

# AT LEAST THE VOICES KEEP ME COMPANY

*God has put the body [of Christ] together such that extra honor and care are given to those parts that have less dignity. This makes for harmony among the members, so that all the members care for each other. If one part suffers, all the parts suffer with it. . . .*
1 Corinthians 12:24–26

I hope and pray you've realized you are not alone. Bible heroes as well as more recent saints struggled with mental health. They were as messed up as you and me! Depression. Bipolar disorder. Suicidal ideation. Post-traumatic stress disorder. And these were people who had an intimate relationship with God. So, as I wrote, mental health issues are not a spiritual issue. (More about that later.)

## Not safe for church

"The Mental & Emotional Health of Pastors and Their Congregants Amid COVID-19," a Barna research study, revealed that only 30 percent of pastors feel well-equipped to help congregants deal with matters of mental or emotional health.

A show of hands, please. How many of you, who have dared to share your mental health issue with a church group, were told to simply pray about it, have more faith, or confess some hidden sin that is causing the issue. (I'm guessing you have your hand up, right?)

We have progressed beyond blaming demons and full moons* for causing mental health issues. And we no longer lock family members in the attic. But we haven't progressed much further! There is still a stigma and suspicion that something is wrong spiritually with anyone with mental health issues.

Sadly, the same study revealed that Christians are half as likely than unbelievers to seek counseling and professional help for mental health issues. One respondent wrote, "Within the Christian community, there is a thick stigma against seeking treatment for mental health, and until this past fall, I found myself convinced that going to counseling was evidence of a lack of faith. I thought that by admitting I needed help for my anxiety and depression I was being sinful."

Fortunately, there is a growing number of books and seminars addressing ministering to those of us with mental health issues. (We've included a list of faith-based resources in the Appendix.) So, carefully seek out those who will accept and assist you.

* We get the label "lunatic" from Latin for moon. While three-fourths of American's believe full moons increase abnormal behavior, a review of more than ten thousand medical records found no relationship between the two. Unfortunately, the study did not address the issue of werewolves.

## PRESCRIPTION

Hillary sat in my office recounting story after story of the wrongs she had done. She had slept around and had always cheated on the people she was in a relationship with. Her current life was full of difficult circumstances, some of her own doing and others because of the wrongs that were done to her. She viewed getting raped, being sexually abused, and taken advantage of throughout her life as a punishment from God. "It was all my fault."

She concluded there on my couch, "God is punishing me." My heart broke to think that somewhere along the line in Sunday school, church, or talking with other Christians she had come to believe some very faulty beliefs about God and his character. Her view of God was that of a lightning bolt-wielding bounty hunter who took great pleasure in destroying her.

Unfortunately, Hillary is not alone in her faulty beliefs about God and her emotions and mental health. We can see from the statistics that the church as a whole has not done well to help those who have trauma, mental illness, emotional issues, or all of the above. In fact, they have instilled some very faulty beliefs into our minds in the name of Jesus. Our challenge today is to identify the lies and misconceptions and replace them with life-giving, realistic, healing truths.

"Other Christians don't feel this way. Something must be wrong with me."

"A good, healthy, strong Christian wouldn't feel this way."

"Good people don't get angry."

"I don't need to deal with my past. I just need to forget it and move on."

"I'm wrong for feeling this way. I must not be trusting God as I should."

"Emotions like hurt, fear, and anger are destructive and dangerous, even sinful."

"If I tell others how I feel, they will think I'm sinful, and not a Christian."

Not only are every one of these statements false, but they also cause more hurt and pain to those of us who are suffering from mental health issues.

☐ **Make a list of long-held, unhelpful beliefs. Shine the light of truth on them**

Write this list in your journal. I'll help you with the first one.

> Belief: "Other Christians don't feel this way. Something must be wrong with me."
>
> Truth: There are thousands of believers in the church struggling with these same issues. I am not alone.

If you are struggling to challenge these beliefs—and you can't think of a true statement—simply leave a blank after Truth. I promise you'll be able to come back later and fill in the blank with confidence if you keep reading.

# 4

# I THINK I AM WHAT I THINK OTHERS THINK I AM

*Become wise by walking with the wise; hang out with fools*
*and watch your life fall to pieces.*
Proverbs 13:20

I still remember some of my Psych 101 professor's one-liners. He was a great teacher and a bit of a comic. Some of his classic quips:

We're all crazy. It's just a matter of degree.

Neurotics *build* castles in the sky. Psychotics *live in* castles in the sky. Psychiatrists collect the rent.

I think I am what I think others think I am.

That last one took a while to think through.

Famous psychologist Erik Erikson believed our self-identity was formed during our adolescent years. However, many other studies show that by the age of three, children have developed a sense of what category into which they fit. They think in terms of young/old, boy/girl, short/tall. Johnny may describe himself as a four-year-old boy with brown eyes, bigger and stronger than his baby sister.

As they grow older, they become aware of an inner self made of emotions and thoughts kept mostly to themselves. Likes and dislikes become formed toward broccoli, pre-school, TV shows, clothing, music, and so on.

Erikson noted eight conflicts we experience at different stages of life. In adolescence, he believed the conflict is "identity versus role confusion."

If you've ever been a teenager, you know the tumultuous struggle you faced with your identity. "I'm no longer my parent's child, but who am I? Why don't I look like the teens on TikTok? What do I really believe about religion and politics? Where am I in the social pecking order?

Ego identity glues all these different identities into a not-so cohesive whole. Think of it as Dr. Frankenstein sewing together various parts of the adolescent. Yeah, that's frightening, but so true.

As I took a graduate class in Social Persuasion, I was shocked to learn that who I thought I was had been indelibly shaped by my parents, Sunday school,* my schoolmates, the media I consumed, and society in general. Shocked and frightened. Human beings are so easily manipulated!

This is why it is so important we surround ourselves with positive role models. Because, as my psychology professor observed, "I think I am what I think others think I am."

And it's why the apostle Paul encouraged his church members:

> Don't copy the behavior and customs of this world, but let God transform you into a new person by changing the way you think. . . .
> Don't think you are better than you really are. Be honest in your evaluation of yourselves, measuring your- selves by the faith God has given us (Romans 12:2–3).

A lot of us don't think much of ourselves. And let's be honest, okay? Many people with mental health issues are often forced to the edges of society. And we're called a lot of names. I get that.

But we need to be thinking of what *God* thinks about us.

* When I was a child, my pastor traumatized me by claiming if I were

the only person on earth, Jesus would have come and died for me. What?! That meant I would have had to kill Jesus?! Yikes! Just another example of how the Church scarred my psyche!

## PRESCRIPTION

Here are some practical ways to begin to have a realistic and biblical view of who you are despite what others may say.

☐ **Do an honest evaluation**

Is there any part of what they said that can be used to grow or change into the person you want to be? What can you learn to have more loving, considerate, and life-giving interactions with others? If your conclusion is that their accusations and assessments are *not* true or accurate at all, move to the next step.

☐ **Consider the source**

Determine whether this is someone's opinion that should matter to you in the grand scheme of things. Is this someone who truly knows you and your heart? If they aren't involved in your life enough that they know your intentions, then they shouldn't be influencing the way you think of yourself, your emotions, or your behaviors.

☐ **Turn the evidence into self-affirmations**

Declare the truth of the evidence to yourself as a self-affirmation: "I am a helpful person because . . ." "I am a great mom because . . ." "They don't know me and my heart." Or "Their opinion of me doesn't matter." "I am blessed to have some amazing, life-giving people in my life." Turn that truthful evidence into your own cheering section.

☐ **Focus on what God says about you**

By the end of this book, you will be equipped with the ability to do an *honest evaluation* of yourself. Paul taught, "Be honest in your evaluation of yourselves, measuring yourselves by the faith God has given us" (Romans 12:3). So, see yourself for who you are through Christ's eyes. God knows you better than anyone, even yourself!

Thumb through the book and look for "Zac" and the ten affirmations. Most important say, I know I am what I know God says I am!

# II

# I AM LOVED

*We know how dearly God loves us, because he has given us the Holy Spirit to fill our hearts with his love.*

Romans 5:5

# 5

# "HI, I'M 'THAT WOMAN'"

*"This is my commandment: Love each other
in the same way I have loved you."*
John 15:12

The weekly Shalom Support Group had gathered for coffee and *suf-ganiyot.** The door quietly opened as a veiled figure tried to find a seat without anyone noticing.

"Welcome," the host announced. "We are so glad to have you join us today."

She quickly sat down and bowed her head.

"Would you please let us know who we have the privilege of welcoming to our group?"

With her head still bent almost to her knees, she whispered, "I'm simply known at 'that woman.' Well, that's the kindest name I'm called. Mostly, it's 'that whore' or 'that woman with seven husbands.'"

Empathetic sighs filled the room.

"Well, be assured that no one here is perfect and that you are safe here. We all love Jehovah and we love you.

She kept her head down. "Some call me Photine,* and I guess I'm a sex addict. It's true, I have had seven husbands and now am living with one who is not my husband." Her body began to convulse. "I just want to be loved."

"Well, you have come to the right place."

Like so many people then and now, she was looking for a genuine love. In 1986, English rocker Steve Winwood won two Grammy awards searching for a "Higher Love." In 30 AD, Jesus taught there is an even *higher* Wynwood love!

### High love

First, he taught, "'You must love the Lord your God with all your heart, all your soul, and all your mind.' This is the first and greatest commandment. A second is equally important: 'Love your neighbor as yourself'" (Matthew 22:37–39).

That commandment went all the way back to the time of Moses and was an essential teaching of the Jewish people. It's the basis of Judeo/Christian belief.

But Jesus raised the bar and called for a . . .

### Higher love

"You have heard the law that says, 'Love your neighbor' and hate your enemy. But I say, love your enemies! Pray for those who persecute you!" (Matthew 5:43–44).

What?! Yeah, I should probably love the person who is like me and lives next door to me. But love those who don't look like me? Those who don't vote like me? Those with whom I share mutual distrust or worst?

Yep. That is a higher love.

But Jesus wasn't done. Not only did he say I should love my neighbor—and my enemy—as I love *myself* but he commands the . . .

### Highest love

"This is my commandment: Love each other in *the same way I have loved you*" (John 15:12, *italics* added).

To love like Jesus?! Yep, and God gives us the power to do exactly that!

Dear friends, since God loved us that much, we surely
ought to love each other. No one has ever seen God. But if

we love each other, God lives in us, and his love is brought
to full expression in us (1 John 4:10–12).

We know how dearly God loves us, because he has
given us the Holy Spirit to fill our hearts with his love"
(Romans 5:5b).

That's a much "Higher Love." It all starts with a relationship with
God who loves us with the highest love. Jesus said:

"For this is how God loved the world: He gave his one and only Son,
so that everyone who believes in him will not perish but have eternal life"
(John 3:16).

* Deep-fried jelly donuts served during Hanukkah

** The woman at the well is given the name Phontine by the Eastern
Orthodox and Eastern Catholic Churches. In Greek, it means "light bearer,"
which is so appropriate since her light led many to believe in Christ.

## PRESCRIPTION

When we're struggling with mental health issues, it's hard to love others, much less ourselves. We want to isolate ourselves from others in our
shame. We get irritable and short with those closest to us. In our isolation,
we get very much in our heads, and we stir up a destructive concoction of
self-hate, guilt, and shame.

☐ **Learn to love yourself**
We must first learn to love ourselves the way God loves us so that
it ripples out into love for others—even our enemies. For this prescription, let's look at Exodus 34:6–7 to read more about God's
"higher love."

Yahweh! The Lord!
The God of compassion and mercy!
I am slow to anger
and filled with unfailing love and faithfulness.
I lavish unfailing love to a thousand generations.
I forgive iniquity, rebellion, and sin.

**God says, "I am the God of compassion and mercy!"** We often say: "I'm worthless. I'm a mistake. I've messed up too many times." Let's love ourselves: "I made a mistake, but I can learn from this and do things differently." Let's love others: "Neither of us is perfect. Let's work together to be better people."

**God says, "I am slow to anger."** We often say: "Ugh! I'm an idiot. I can't believe I did that. How stupid can I be?" Let's love ourselves: "I need to stop beating myself up all the time. I need to learn self-compassion." Let's love others: "You hurt me, but I don't want to act on my anger or be an angry, bitter person."

**God says, "I am filled with unfailing love and faithfulness."** We often say: "I hate myself. I'm a terrible person." Let's love ourselves: "God, help me to love myself as you love me." Let's love others: "Yes they hurt me, but I can begin the healing in myself by loving as Jesus loves."

God is the Lord of compassion and mercy, slow to anger, filled with unfailing love and faithfulness, and forgives freely. Let's ask him to help us to change our thoughts and beliefs in order to love more like him. As he helps us to change our thoughts and beliefs about ourselves and others, our emotions will follow suit. When we give ourselves and others compassion and mercy, we can easily forgive ourselves and others and let go of guilt and shame. Being kinder to ourselves and others through our thoughts, words, and actions will help us to offer grace and let go of hurts and resentments. We will love others more deeply and genuinely, and we will find healing in our hearts. Learning to love ourselves and others helps us to love God more perfectly and practice forgiveness.

☐ Practice flipping the script in your heart and thoughts in order to more readily show compassion and mercy and to love and forgive ourselves and others.

☐ Pray: "God of compassion and mercy, help me love myself so I am free to love you, my neighbor, and even my enemies."

# 6

# LOOKIN' FOR LOVE IN ALL THE *RIGHT* PLACES

*Dear friends, since God loved us that much, we surely ought to love*
*each other. No one has ever seen God. But if we love each other,*
*God lives in us, and his love is brought to full expression in us.*
1 John 4:11–12

Kevin and Jennifer sincerely want to please God. But both are discouraged. Kevin has "committed," "recommitted," "totally committed," and "totally recommitted" his life to Christ—at least a half dozen times. He's really trying to live a disciplined life for the Lord, but it seems he fails daily.

Jennifer really trusts God to work through her. "Hey, just keep in the Spirit and let the Holy Ghost have his way!" But she, too, seems to find herself with the wrong crowd doing the wrong things.

Kevin believes living a life pleasing to God comes from discipline and commitment. He's right. Jennifer believes pleasing God is a gift from him that we ask for in faith. And she's right. But both are only half right. Living a holy or "sanctified" life comes through a *combination* of our willpower and his power.

In fact, the word "sanctification" has a two-part meaning: set apart for holy use and cleansed.

## Our part

Let's say a priest wanted to sanctify a bowl for use in the Jewish Temple. That bowl was dedicated for Temple use—and only for Temple use.

Never again could it be used to serve tortilla chips, pot a fern, or set under the chariot when he changed the oil. It was only for God's usage. The priest then gave it a good scrubbing and set it in the Temple.

In the same way, we need to set ourselves apart for God's sole use. That's the human element in sanctification—or as John Wesley called it "perfect love."* (That sounds less stuffy and theological!) God helps us see the joy and privileges we're missing by not experiencing perfect love. He will show us areas that need his lordship. But he can't dedicate us to himself. That's our part.

## God's part

God first loved us and sent his Son to buy us back (John 3:16, Romans 5:6–8), and sent his Spirit to show us we need his salvation (John 16:8). He loves us, reveals himself to us, and convicts us of our sins.

But that's as far as God will go, unless we confess our sins, believe on him, and repent (Acts 2:38).

But once we do, he eagerly forgives us (Acts 2:38), makes us a new creation (2 Corinthians 5:17), adopts us as his kids (Romans 8:14, 15), and gives us his Spirit to live inside us. We accept all this by faith.

Unfortunately, that's where many Christians stop. But in Romans 12:1 and 2, Paul writes to his Christian friends:

> And so, dear brothers and sisters, I plead with you to give your bodies to God because of all he has done for you. Let them be a living and holy sacrifice—the kind he will find acceptable. This is truly the way to worship him. Don't copy the behavior and customs of this world, but let God transform you into a new person by changing the way you think. Then you will learn to know God's will for you, which is good and pleasing and perfect.

Paul writes about people with "Their minds are full of darkness; they wander far from the life God gives because they have closed their minds and hardened their hearts against him" (Ephesians 4:18). But, the apostle John writes, "The blood of Jesus, his Son, purifies us from all sin" (1 John 1:7). The first step to experiencing God's perfect love is salvation.

However, the next step "setting ourselves apart for holy use" is strictly our part. Yes, God will give us the power and wisdom to live a holy life, but he will never set us apart. That's our responsibility!

So, here's the takeaway: "Let God transform you into a new person by the way you think" (Romans 12:2). But you must allow him to.

\* The phrase "perfect love" is found in 1 John 4:4: "Perfect love expels all fear."

## PRESCRIPTION

I've been a licensed clinical addictions counselor for twenty years, so this idea of being set apart and cleansed made me immediately think of the process of change in twelve-step recovery programs, more precisely the first four steps, which I've paraphrased:

☐ **I admit I am powerless over [fill in the blank] and that my life has become unmanageable**
Are there any areas in your life that feel out of control for you in your life? List in your journal areas of your life where you feel helpless and lost. Don't feel overwhelmed. Remember, this book is all about hope!

☐ **I believe that a Power greater than myself can restore me to sanity**
Re-read Acts 2:38. Read Romans 10:9-10.

☐ **I make a decision to turn my will and my life over to the care of God**
These two go hand in hand. If we believe that God, who lavishes us with his love, can heal us, and help us in the really difficult places to control, we are then willing to give ourselves to him. We must let go of the belief

that we can do everything on our own and surrender ourselves into the hands of the One who can truly change our hearts and minds.

We set ourselves apart by allowing God, the one who loves us, to walk through these challenges with us. Do you believe that he can change you, and are you willing to be set apart and surrender into his loving hands?

☐ **I search myself and make a fearless moral inventory of myself**
This step takes us on a deep dive into our soul to search out what is keeping us stuck and leading to our own demise. Are there deep-down beliefs, attitudes, thoughts, emotions, urges, and behaviors that are keeping you stuck? As God shows you these things, write them in your journal. Although it feels daunting, remember Paul knew this struggle well: "Let God transform you into a new person by the way you think." (Romans 12:2). The transformation will come, but first, we have to do the ABCDs of our part, Admit, Believe, Commit, and Do the work. Together with him, and perhaps a trusted therapist, you *can* do it!

☐ **Pray: "You will faithfully do your part, Lord. Help me do my part in becoming conformed into your likeness"**

# 7

# I'M NOT PARAGRAPH 315.1 IN *THE DSM*

*I am all too human. . . . I don't really understand myself.*
Romans 6:14

T*he Diagnostic and Statistical Manual of Mental Health*\* is a publication by the American Psychiatric Association (APA) for the classification of mental health disorders. It groups various diagnoses into five broad categories:

1. Anxiety disorders
2. Bipolar and related disorders
3. Depressive disorders
4. Feeding and eating disorders
5. Obsessive-compulsive and related disorders
6. Personality disorders

For instance, sub-category 315.1 in the chapter title is something called "Mathematics Disorder." It deals with dyscalculia, sometimes called dysarithmia. According to Dyscalculia.org, it is—and I quote—"a math learning disorder that makes mathematical reasoning and computation difficult, in spite of adequate education, average or greater intelligence, and proper motivation."

Yep, that was me in high school! I was doing well with X, but then they threw in Y and Z, and I quickly learned the part of my brain that is supposed to do higher math is MIA!

In an age that cancels anyone who categorizes people by race, gender, sexual orientation, creed, national origin, or whether they prefer Coke or Pepsi, the *DSM-V* has been criticized by many mental health professionals since the first edition back in 1952.

The most common complaint is its use of arbitrary dividing lines between mental illness and "normality." (Yeah, that can be a very thin line.) Dr. Allen Frances of Duke University School of Medicine has gone on record claiming that because of the *DSM* "normality is an endangered species," due to "fad diagnoses" and an "epidemic" of over-diagnosing.

He went on to warn in a 2012 blog post at PsychologyToday.com of "potentially harmful changes" in lumping normal grief into the category of a Major Depressive Disorder, labeling "normal forgetfulness in old age" as Minor Neurocognitive Disorder, and calling "everything we like to do a lot" Behavioral Addictions. Apparently, my love for writing is a Behavioral Addiction. (Well, writers *are* a peculiar people!)

I have a college minor in Psychology, which means I know just enough to be dangerous. (Never fear, my daughter will correct any mental health heresy.) But here's my point:

## Mental health is not binary

It's not 0 or 1, black or white, or yes or no. Think of it as a spectrum. You're not a sane saint or an insane psychopath, but somewhere in between. It's like the famous bell curve. Most people fall in the middle, with Mother Teresa and Adolph Hitler on the opposite extremes. I would like to think I'm closer to the modern-day saint than the misogynistic madman, but I have to admit I'm no saint. The best we can say is it's complicated.

The apostle Paul writes about his contradictory desires:

> So the trouble is not with the law, for it is spiritual
> and good. The trouble is with me, for I am all too human,
> a slave to sin. I don't really understand myself, for I want
> to do what is right, but I don't do it. Instead, I do what I

hate. But if I know that what I am doing is wrong, this shows that I agree that the law is good (Romans 6:14–16).

And he questions his mixed motives:

> As for me, it matters very little how I might be evaluated by you or by any human authority. I don't even trust my own judgment on this point. My conscience is clear, but that doesn't prove I'm right. It is the Lord himself who will examine me and decide (1 Corinthians 4:3–4).

There's even an online message board that attempts to psychoanalyze Paul!

## We are not a number in the DSM

But here's my most important point: The *DSM-V* is perfect for categorizing people for insurance claim purposes, but people are much too complex to fit into even the hundreds of categories and sub-categories in the book. Instead, God loves and knows each of us as unique individuals. We're not a number, although he does know the number of hairs on their heads (Luke 12:7).

> O Lord, you have examined my heart and know everything about me (Psalm 139:1).

> "I know every thought that comes into your minds" (The Lord, Ezekiel 11:5).

> The Lord is good, a stronghold in the day of trouble; he knows those who take refuge in him (Nahum 1:7 ESV).

> "I knew you before I formed you in your mother's womb" (Jeremiah 1:5).

"I am the good shepherd; I know my own sheep, and they know me" (Jesus, John 10:14).

So, I am not a category or even a thousand sub-categories. I am James Nathan Watkins, a beloved child of God. That's my classification. I pray it's yours!

* Please don't go to the *DSM* online and attempt to diagnose yourself. That's dangerous. You're planning to Google it right now, aren't you? Seriously, you may convince yourself you have hundreds of psychoses. You're still planning to do it?! Take this book and repeatedly smack your forehead until the desire passes.

## PRESCRIPTION

I usually begin a client's first session with, "So tell me, what makes you *you*?" The typical response is a deer-in-the-headlights look. Perhaps they feel it's just a loaded question, or they weren't expecting it. Or perhaps my clients have gotten so bogged down with their current emotional state that they have forgotten that the sum of who they are is far greater than their current problem or symptoms that brought them to therapy. Soon the uneasiness begins to fade, and that one simple question opens up Pandora's box of all things they love, people they love, things they love to do, the various roles they play, and their dreams and passions. I love getting to know the whole person sitting in front of me who is uniquely gifted and created for a purpose. I want my clients to see this whole-person view of themselves too.

So what makes Faith *Faith*? I'm a mom. I'm a therapist and a writer. I love people deeply, I'm compassionate and thoughtful. I am faithful and loyal, sometimes to a fault. I love to travel and make memories with my daughters. And I am the daughter of the Creator of the universe, and I am deeply loved by him.

So, "What makes you *you*?" Be sure to include "I am fearfully and wonderfully made. I am a child of the Creator of the universe, and I am deeply loved by him."

☐ **Take some time to sit in a quiet space and contemplate the question "What makes me *me*?" Then start writing and let your pen take you away.**

# 8

# MOOD-ALTERING HUGS

*A time to embrace.*
Ecclesiastes 3:5

Methylenedioxymethamphetamine goes by the name of MDMA or "Ecstasy" and sometimes "the Hug Drug."

The hug drug is classified as a psychotropic or "mood-altering" drug. Other drugs in this category include antidepressants, cocaine, heroin, LSD, marijuana, nicotine, Ritalin, and caffeine (I always feel much better after massive doses of dark chocolate).

Nasty side effects of the hug drug include dizziness, nausea, confusion, and hallucinations. It's considered "extremely dangerous," so I'm not pushing its use.

I am, however, pushing a perfectly safe alternative to the hug drug: hugs. Real hugs—not drugs—are actually good for your health. According to social scientist Virginia Satir, "You need four hugs a day for survival, eight for maintenance, and twelve for growth." [*]

John Naisbitt also praised hugs in his 1982 best-seller *Megatrends*. One of the trends he predicted was an emphasis on "High Tech/High Touch." "In a world of technology, people long for personal, human contact."

Kathleen Keating Schloessinger, R.N., M.A., has also written a best-seller on the subject, *The Hug Therapy Book* (CompCare Publishers, 1983).

We are suffering in our society from a sad condition best described as touch deprivation, skin hunger, and hug inhibition. We need to recognize that every human being has a profound physical and emotional need for touch—men and women and children. And even our animal companions!

Scientific research has shown that hugging makes us feel better about ourselves and our surroundings, has a positive effect on a child's development and IQ, and causes measurable physiological changes in the hugger and hug-ee. (Research has also documented the physical and psychological damage to children who were not held and hugged as infants.)

Of course, Internet nitwits were quick to exploit this phenomenon. One site offers, and I quote:

> Hug Therapy! For a mere $15 per half hour, you can experience total release and contentment through the simple, yet rare, experience of human contact. Our professional team is trained in a variety of hug-therapy techniques and will be happy to guide you to a land of decompression.

I emailed for details and received several offers for less than platonic body contact.

Nonsexual hugging has some major advantages over "the hug drug" and other mood-altering drugs.

A hug is free. It's beneficial physically and emotionally, with absolutely no adverse side effects (unless you're being hugged by a bear or professional wrestler). It's energy efficient, ecological sound, and requires no special equipment or training, licenses, prescriptions, tax forms, dealer prep, or destination charges. And, unlike high- tech equipment, hugs never need recharging, don't come with a three-hundred-page instruction manual, and never, ever lock up or crash.

So get high on hugs—not drugs.

\* From the publisher's lawyer: Do *not* hug random strangers! The authors and publisher of this book are not responsible for any legal action including but not limited to restraining orders that may result from any unwanted contact.

## PRESCRIPTION

Today's reading took me back to my years away at university. I was over an hour away from home and without my daily dose of hugs from my parents, I started to notice that I was going through serious "hug withdrawal." For my high school graduation, I had been given back support pillow with arms. While away from home, it became more than just a pillow to support me while I sat in bed studying late at night. When I was feeling lonely, sad, overwhelmed, or homesick, I went to my "God pillow" as I referred to it, and pretended I was crawling into God's lap and the arms of the pillow became his strong, loving embrace.

Even twenty-plus years after graduating from college, I still find myself hug-deprived. I'm a single mom of teenagers, so that means no man to meet that need, and my girls who used to be huge huggers now immediately stand stiff as a board as if disgusted that I am coming in for an embrace. So, what's one to do? We can't just go around hugging random strangers or hugging every little child that we see. The following are some ways to meet physical touch needs when it may not be socially acceptable and frowned upon to do so. As much as I love hugs, you won't find me out in public wearing a "Free Hugs" shirt.

☐ **Hug yourself**
Seriously. Cross your arms and give yourself a huge squeeze and say to yourself, "I love you. You are an amazing person and worthy of hugs."

☐ **Hug a friend**
Since being armed with the knowledge that single people struggle to get their daily hug quota met, when I do hug a friend, I hold on just a little longer and tighter, but not too long. That would just be awkward.

☐ **Hug your pet**

Unfortunately, my dog isn't really the snuggling type, but sometimes when I feel the need, I'll just randomly pick him up and say, "Milo, Mommy needs a hug." And I'll just stand and hold him for a few minutes. He always makes me feel loved.

☐ **Hug a pillow**

Hear me out! In writing this, I had to Google to find out the actual name for my pillow with the arms, and one site referred to it as a "husband pillow." So maybe it's time to buy such a pillow to curl up with after a long difficult day. Hugging a body pillow, resting under a weighted blanket, and wrapping up in a soft fluffy bathrobe are also ways to feel comforted. Or for those of you with a spouse or kids who love to hug, that's even better.

☐ **Choose some kind of hug-like activity this week, and treat yourself to the healing power of a hug**

# III

# I AM SEEN

*You saw me before I was born. Every day of my life
was recorded in your book. Every moment was laid out
before a single day had passed. How precious
are your thoughts about me, O God.
They cannot be numbered!*

Psalm 139:16–17

# 9

# "HI, I'M HAGAR. I'M HOMELESS"

*Hagar used another name to refer to the Lord, who had spoken to her. She said, "You are the God who sees me."*
Genesis 16:13

"Hi and welcome to our third meeting of the Shalom Support Group. Many of you probably know our first-timer, Hagar."

Everyone around the circle nodded their heads. It seemed everyone knew the scandalous story of Abram and Sarai's attempt to have a child through, shall we say, a "surrogate."

"Now I'm pregnant, scorned, and homeless!"

"Well, you have come to the right place. We have found a place where we are recognized and cared for."

Photine stood and gave Hagar a big hug. "Definitely, Hagar. I can relate, so let's go out for coffee and falafels after the meeting?"

As you may remember, God had promised Abram and Sarai a child, although she had been barren and now was well past the hot-flash stage of life. (The couple changed their names after the birth of their firs born, so yeah, it's the same two: Abraham and Sarah.)

In Genesis 12, God promises the *seventy-five-year-old* Abram not only a child but a "great nation." God reminds him of the promise later in Genesis 15:5: "Then the Lord took Abram outside and said to him, 'Look up into the sky and count the stars if you can. That's how many descendants you will have!'"

But now, Abram and Sarai have been waiting ten years for this promised birth. And so, like a lot of humans, Sarai decides God needs some help!

> So Sarai said to Abram, "The Lord has prevented me from having children. Go and sleep with my servant. Perhaps I can have children through her." And Abram agreed with Sarai's proposal. So Sarai, Abram's wife, took Hagar the Egyptian servant and gave her to Abram as a wife (16:2–3).

And of course, when you try to help God, it ends up as a Titanic Hindenburg of a train wreck. Hagar starts taunting that she's preggers and Sarai is not. Sarai retaliates and treats Hagar "harshly." So, mom-to-be escapes to the desert!

Hagar felt alone, rejected, unseen, and very pregnant! This is no fault of her own since slaves were regarded as property that could be used and abused—and even forced to marry an old man.* This is not the happy marriage she had been dreaming about since a girl.

But God sees her and sends his angel to comfort her.

Fun fact: This is the first time in Scripture a person encounters the "Angel of the Lord." And she's a lowly Egyptian slave girl, not a member of God's "chosen people." But wait, there's more: Scholars believe this is not just any angel but the "Angel of God's Presence"—Jesus Christ, the Son of God, himself! Wow.

Out of this soap opera of conflict comes comfort in Genesis 16:13.

"Hagar used another name to refer to the Lord, who had spoken to her. She said, 'You are the God who sees me.'"

I love that! Each of us has stories of where our mental health issues have caused us to feel unseen. Maybe you were not invited to birthday parties as a child. Maybe you had trouble dating. You didn't even get the pity of "Well, they have a nice personality." Nope! You have multiple personalities! Maybe you didn't get the job you dreamed of. You were overlooked for promotion. (Corporate wants compliant, not "quirky.")

So, no sappy, pat answer here! Sometimes we are ignored. Avoided.

Shunned. For no fault of our own except messed up brain chemistry or a traumatic childhood.

But Faith and I see you.** And more importantly, God sees you!

* I love, love, love the way Jesus treats women! In that culture, Jewish men daily thanked God they had not been born a Gentile, a dog, or a woman. (Notice the order.) A man never spoke to a woman in public, women were not allowed an education, and they were banned from testifying in court due to their mental "instability." So, what did Jesus do? He spoke to the woman at the well, recruited female disciples, and entrusted Mary Magdalene to testify to the greatest event in history: his resurrection!

** Figuratively, of course, because stalking you would be just wrong.

## PRESCRIPTION

Hagar's story has personally spoken to my heart during those dark nights of the soul when I felt so alone and no one could ever understand the hell I was going through. Hagar's story reminds me that despite my feelings of loneliness, God, the creator of the universe and the creator of my soul, sees me and knows every single ounce of my pain. The God of the universe sees you right where you are at this exact moment.

My dad put the following verses together to encourage you that God sees you. And I want to help you make them more personal for you and your situation.

☐ **Do you feel misunderstood?**

Do you struggle to even understand yourself and your circumstances?

"But as for me, LORD, you know my heart. You see me and test my thoughts" (Jeremiah 12:3).

☐ **Do you feel lonely and unloved?**

"But the Lord watches over those who fear him, those who rely on his unfailing love" (Psalm 33:18).

☐ **Do you feel unworthy, insignificant, or worthless?**

"I knew you before I formed you in your mother's womb. Before you were born I set you apart and appointed you as my prophet to the nations" (Jeremiah 1:5).

☐ **Do you feel overwhelmed and tired with nothing left to give?**

"The eyes of the Lord search the whole earth in order to strengthen those whose hearts are fully committed to him (2 Chronicles 16:9).

☐ **Are you so full of fear and anxiety you feel like you can't go on?**

"Don't be afraid, for I am with you. Don't be discouraged, for I am your God. I will strengthen you and help you. I will hold you up with my victorious right hand" (Isaiah 41:10).

☐ **Do you feel unseen and rejected as Hagar did?**

The Lord keeps watch over you as you come and go, both now and forever (Psalm 121:8).

☐ **If you can relate to any of these situations, I encourage you to write the particular verse out on a three-by-five card or post it, and put it somewhere where you can remember its comforting truth when your feelings tell you that you are unseen**

# 10

# I FEEL LOCKED
# IN THE ATTIC

*Some parts of the body [of Christ] that seem weakest and least
important are actually the most necessary. And the parts we
regard as less honorable are those we clothe with the greatest
care. So we carefully protect those parts that should not be seen,
while the more honorable parts do not require this special care.
So God has put the body together such that extra honor and care
are given to those parts that have less dignity.*
1 Corinthians 12:22–24

Do you ever feel unimportant? Dishonored? Socially isolated? Treated
with little dignity? Apparently, that was a problem at the First Church
of Corinth. And virtually every church around the world has one or more
such people. Those with mental health issues are no longer locked up in
the attic, but they are socially just as hidden and isolated.

I volunteered for ten years at the welcome desk of a growing church
answering questions, giving direction, and handing out free mugs to visitors,
but most of all I was a "noticer."

And in that role, I had the opportunity to provide "special care" to a
group of about ten mentally-challenged adults and children. These were
God's children who just happened to have clinical depression, bipolar disorder, autism, and developmental issues, and one I'm pretty sure was psychotic
by the conflicting stories he told of being married to a Hollywood actress.

Each would stop by every Sunday just to be noticed. It was an honor to
serve them!

Francis of Assisi (circa 1182-1226) was probably living somewhere along the autism spectrum or as it was called several years ago: Asperger's Syndrome. He was highly intelligent but also highly eccentric. He was best known for his love and compassion for all of God's creatures.*

The Church at the time labeled Francis a fool and a clown for his "holy folly" in embracing poverty with such joy. In establishing hundreds of groups of professional clergy and laity to serve the poor, he faithfully lived out the apostle Paul's testimony: "Our dedication to Christ makes us look like fools" (1 Corinthians 4:10).

A Freudian psychiatrist would attribute his compassionate characteristics to an attempt to deal with what would be known today as Post-Traumatic Stress Disorder. Francis served in combat against an Italian dissident group where he saw life-long friends torn limb from limb in gruesome fighting. He was captured as a POW and imprisoned for one year in what was not much more than a dark, dank hole in the ground.

One of Francis' biographers, Thomas of Celano, reports that once released, he felt nothing when he looked at fields and mountains that once thrilled and inspired him. Celano describes him as a broken man, who was too physically and emotionally weak as well as depressed to venture out of his house. A close study of Francis' writing reveals that the "dark shadows" and "demons" never completely disappeared.

But God saw Francis of Assisi and used him in remarkable ways to create and establish charitable and missionary organizations throughout the world today. Like Frances, you belong!

* Francis of Assisi did *not* write "Make Me an Instrument of Your Peace." Shocking isn't it? The essay was actually was written in 1912—nearly seven hundred years after his death.

## PRESCRIPTION

One of the many questions that I ask when I first meet with a client is: What are your strengths? Sadly, a very common response is, "I don't have

any." Life has beaten them down to the point where they see nothing positive about themselves. What about you? Are you able to see your positive
qualities, assets, or skills? What are they? And you aren't allowed to say,
"Not applicable" because we all have strengths that were infused into our
being while being knit together in our mother's womb. If you are struggling to identify your strengths, ask a close friend or someone you trust to
articulate to you the strengths and assets that they see in you. Write them
in your journal.

The Holy Spirit dwells within us and has gifted us with spiritual gifts
to build his Kingdom.

☐ **What are my spiritual gifts?**

I recommend finding a free spiritual gifts assessment online to help
you identify your spiritual gifts. God has made you beautifully and
wonderfully unique, and he has gifted you with strengths and spiritual
gifts that can join forces to change the world around you. When you
discover them, write them in your journal.

☐ **How can I employ my spiritual gifts?**

I have God-given care and concern for others, see the best in people,
and have the spiritual gifting of encouragement and teaching, along
with my dark seasons filled with hurt and pain and the healing I have
experienced. So, all these things combine to create my superpower of
sitting with others in their pain and offering insights, strategies, encouragement, and comfort in the darkest of places. It is such an honor to use
my strengths. Ask God to help you find specific and practical ways to
use the gifts he has given you to lead others to him.

# 11

# I AM SEEN AND CELEBRATED

*For the Lord your God is living among you. He is a mighty savior.*
*He will take delight in you with gladness. With his love, he will*
*calm all your fears. He will rejoice over you with joyful songs.*
Zephaniah 3:17

You've probably seen someone—when confronted with something truly amazing—put her hands on the side of her head, fling out her arms wide, and exclaim, "Mind blown!"*

Yep, that's how I feel when I read the words of the prophet Zephaniah. Mind blown!

In chapter nine, we learned one of God's many names in Scripture: "The God Who Sees Me." And if that's not amazing enough, the prophet writes that the Creator and Lord of the universe *celebrates* me! He rejoices over me with joyful songs! Yeah, we know that God loves us. That's who he is—love. He can't help but love us. But here, we see that God *likes* us. We bring him joy! Mind blown!

I've often wondered what that song would sound like. What would be the message? We can get a clue by reading what he says about us in his Word:

> I take delight in you with gladness,
> I rejoice over you with joyous song (Zephaniah 3:17).
> You didn't choose me. I chose you (John 15:16).
> I so loved you that I gave my only Son

that believing in him you may have eternal life
(John 3:16).

I showed this great love by sending him

while you were estranged from me by sin (Romans 5:8).

I am with you wherever you go (Joshua 1:9).

I have called you by name; you are mine (Isaiah 43:1).

See, I have written your name on the palms of my
hands (Isaiah 49:16).

See how very much I love you,

for I call you my children, and that is what you are!
(1 John 3:1)

For my Spirit joins with your spirit to affirm that you
are my children.

And since you are my children, you are my heir.

In fact, together with Christ, you are heirs of my glory
(Romans 8:16-17).

I will never abandon you as an orphan (John 14:18).

But now, nothing can separate you from my love,

neither death, life, angels, nor demons.

Neither our fears for today or worries about tomorrow.

No power in the sky or on the earth below can separate
you from my love displayed in Christ (Romans 8:38–39).


Put this song on your mental "playlist." Listen to it daily, and you will
indeed find your mind blown—and comforted—with his love!


* The original meaning of *mind blown* is closely tied to drug use,
especially psychedelic drugs during the 1960s. Like so many things make
a comeback, in the mid/late 2000s, mind blown returned on social media,
but this time meaning something amazing, surprising, or incredible.
(Fortunately, at this time, paisley shirts, polyester leisure suits, and platform shoes have not been resurrected from the fashion graveyard!)

## PRESCRIPTION

When I was going through my divorce and my mind was heavy, I created a playlist of encouraging songs. They filled my heart with peace, courage, and hope as I walked through a very difficult season. It played non-stop in my car for at least six months. Some days, it was just background noise that was drowned out by my anxious, fearful thoughts. Other times, I sang along and belted out every single lyric, boldly proclaiming them, not caring what other motorists might think. And still, there were other days when I listened to the deeper meaning of these songs and just let them saturate my soul with their hope-giving truths.

Listening to these songs on repeat for months at a time began to change my thoughts, my emotions, and my heart. And even today, years later, if I hear one of those songs from my divorce playlist, I can sing every note and lyric without missing a beat, and I'm reminded of the way God healed my heart over those months of listening to that CD.

The beauty of music is that it has the power to change our emotions at any given moment. A song can bring back memories of a loved one and fill us with grief or happy remembrance. When we are feeling down, a song can make us smile, laugh or just get up and dance. Or if we need a good cry, we put on a sad song. Or a heavy metal song can overwhelm and numb our minds and thoughts so that we don't have to think about anything.

Thankfully, we don't have to wait until the radio plays our favorite song to record it or burn a CD anymore. We have millions of songs at our disposal on iTunes, Spotify, Amazon Music, or whatever media player you use.

☐ **Create your own playlist**
Find or make a playlist that reflects your current mood, evokes an emotion that you want to have, or just simply relaxes you after a long day. Music has a magical way of soothing our souls.

☐ **Go back and re-read God's "song" that Dad mixed for you**
What specific lines of these lyrics struck a chord in you? What lines were music to your ears? Which ones made you stop and change your

tune? Circle or underline the specific lines or phrases that spoke to your heart right there where you are today. Write them down in your journal.

Dad's mashup may not be on your favorite music platform, but you can put it on repeat like a broken record in your heart and let these truths soak deep into your soul. And if you are musically inclined, consider writing this into an actual song that can be shared with the rest of us! (Put it on YouTube, send the link to jim@jameswatkins.com, and we'll add it to our Prozac playlist.) Whatever you do, get this song stuck on repeat in the playlist of your mind and have your mind blown—and comforted—with his love!

☐ **Go to jameswatkins.com/prozac and be encouraged by the playlist we've put together just for you**

# 12

# INKBLOTS: BUTTERFLY OR BLOOD SPLATTER?

*So we don't look at the troubles we can see now; rather, we fix our*
*gaze on things that cannot be seen. For the things we see now will*
*soon be gone, but the things we cannot see will last forever.*
2 Corinthians 4:18

We've all seen those Rorschach tests made up of ten cards with ink-blots folded over to create a bisymmetrical image. The one-hundred-dred-year-old test was designed by Swiss psychiatrist Hermann Rorschach. He believed that people who suffer from mental health issues would "project" different meanings on the images than "normal" people would. It's a subjective test, so there are no official right or wrong answers, but test-givers are provided a list of what are called "normed responses."

Patients are supposed to interpret something meaningful from random splotches and thus reveal their deep-seated psychoses.

"Well, it looks like a butterfly, but you probably want me to tell you that I feel trapped in the chrysalis of my addiction to broccoli and I'm seeking to break free of my vegetable obsession and fly like I was created to do!"

But usually, people just say butterfly. However, if I interpret the shape as blood splatter from a serial killer[*] who has just stabbed to death his roommate for not doing his assigned chores, I would earn a seventy-two-hour stay at the local "health spa."

The test's reliability has recently been questioned, but it's clear that how we perceive life depends on our mental health.

God asks us to look at life from his perspective:

> Don't copy the behavior and customs of this world, but let God transform you into a new person by changing the way you think (Romans 12:2a).

> Think about the things of heaven, not the things of earth (Colossians 3:2).

> You will keep in perfect peace all who trust in you, all whose thoughts are fixed on you! (Isaiah 26:3)

> Let the Spirit renew your thoughts and attitudes (Ephesians 4:23).

> Don't worry about anything; instead, pray about everything. Tell God what you need, and thank him for all he has done. Then you will experience God's peace, which exceeds anything we can understand. His peace will guard your hearts and minds as you live in Christ Jesus (Philippians 4:6–7).

I love the story of Elisha in 2 Kings 6. Each time King Ben-hadad of Aram planned an attack on Israel, God would reveal the enemy's strategies to the prophet, so the Hebrew army was always a step ahead. Ben-hadad eventually learned of Elisha's abilities and sent a large number of soldiers with chariots and horses to surround the city where the prophet was hiding.

When Elisha's administrative servant came running in with "We're surrounded! We're going to die!" the prophet casually replied, "Don't be afraid! For there are more on our side than on theirs!" The servant probably looked around as if to say, "Dude, it's just you and me!"

But the Bible records "Elisha prayed, 'O Lord, open his eyes and let him see!' The Lord opened the young man's eyes, and when he looked up, he saw that the hillside around Elisha was filled with horses and chariots of fire" (2 Kings 6:17).

If I truly believe God sees me and is with me through every challenge, I can see life from his perspective. Look for the butterflies and not the blood splatters.

* The one common denominator of all serial killers is they keep a journal. They want to be able to recount their crime with a detailed description. All serial killers journal, but not all who journal are serial killer, so please keep journaling. You do see the butterfly, right?!

## PRESCRIPTION

Let me be clear, Dad isn't talking about having a Pollyanna attitude dripping with sweetness and positivity twenty-four/seven or wearing rose-colored glasses where life is full of sunshine, rainbows, and unicorns. This is *not* a "just think happy thoughts" kind of perspective.

Elisha and the Israelites were in fact in the midst of a pretty dismal situation. Elisha and his servant did not experience a *problem* change at that moment, but his servant had a *perspective* shift. Our thoughts and perspectives by nature tend to be negative and sometimes doomsday-like. That's why Paul talks about our thoughts needing to be transformed and renewed to have an eternal perspective (Romans 12:2).

So how do we have this transformation? Focusing on the truth of Scripture is one way that we have been focusing on throughout our time together. But there is a way to use even our life experiences to help us shift our perspective.

☐ **Think about a dark time in your life that God worked for your good** (Romans 8:28)

Identify a circumstance from your past that seemed really hard at the time, but you have learned and grown from it. At the time how did it feel? Do you feel differently about it now? You may think, *I didn't think I would make it through that season, but I did, and I know I can make it through this one too.* Or, *This won't last forever. I've already been through painful experiences and survived."*

☐ **Ask, "What could the Father be doing in this present difficult time to make me more like his Son?"** (Romans 8:29)

Even when I was overwhelmed with the pain of rejection, unfaithfulness, and divorce, there was a part of me that said, "I don't see it at all right now, but I trust that something good will come out of this." Looking back to that dark season, I had no idea that I would be flourishing, living my best life, writing a book with my dad encouraging others with the healing I have found over the last twelve years.

When you are faced with a difficult experience, you can also think of your future self and how you will see your situation in the future looking back. "Will future me still be stressed about this in twenty years? Will I even remember? Will this matter in five years? Will this even matter next week?"

Even if it feels so dark that you can't even see into next hour, you can know that what you are feeling or experiencing is temporary and short-lived in the light of eternity.

Trust me, it takes a lot of training and practice to change our thoughts and perspective, but start today by capturing those unhelpful catastrophic thoughts. Just as with the lowly little caterpillar, there's a purpose and hope for your life even if you can't see it right now.

# IV

## I AM IMPORTANT

*When we were utterly helpless, Christ came at just the right time and died for us sinners. Now, most people would not be willing to die for an upright person, though someone might perhaps be willing to die for a person who is especially good. But God showed his great love for us by sending Christ to die for us while we were still sinners.*

Romans 5:6-8

# 13

# "HI, I'M GIDEON.
# I'M A NOBODY"

*You are a chosen people. You are royal priests, a holy nation,
God's very own possession. As a result, you can show others
the goodness of God, for he called you out of the darkness
into his wonderful light.*

1 Peter 2:9

"Welcome back to the Shalom Support Group. We want to celebrate each of you and the progress you're making in successfully dealing with your mental health issues. I'm proud of you. So, who would like to go first?"

A hand rose slowly, tentatively.

"Uh . . . Hi, I'm Gideon. And please excuse my wet sheepskin. It's a long story.*

"Anyway, there I was hiding in a winery trying to grind what little wheat I had in a wine vat so the Midianites didn't steal that. They had come into the land, stole all our livestock, destroyed our crops, and left us with nothing to eat. Just as I was thinking how bad things had become, this angel showed up and announced, 'Mighty hero, the LORD is with you!' I looked around to see who this mighty hero he was talking to was, and I'm the only one there!

"So, I just blurted out, 'Sir, if the LORD is with us, why has all this happened to us? And where are all the miracles our ancestors told us about? Didn't they say, "The LORD brought us up out of Egypt?" But now the LORD has abandoned us and handed us over to the Midianites.'

"But he just said, 'Go with the strength you have, and rescue Israel from the Midianites. I am sending you! And you will destroy the Midianites as if you were fighting against one man'" (Judges 6).

The members of the group jumped to their feet and started to applaud and cheer! "Migh-ty warrior! Migh-ty warrior! Migh-ty . . ."

"No! No! That's just crazy! Sorry, that's probably not the best word choice with this group, but that's what it is! Crazy! I'm just an unimportant nobody."

The group collectively shrugged their shoulders and once again shouted, "Migh-ty warrior! Migh-ty warrior! Migh-ty . . ."

Have you ever felt that way? You come from a family with mental health issues—some acknowledged and probably most denied. And now you're becoming aware that you too are becoming just like them. And so, you think, *I'm just a* [fill in an insulting adjective for your condition]. This situation is not going to change. And worse, you may feel abandoned by God.

How we feel about ourselves is so powerful and influential to our mental health it will determine if we deal with it or just go on ignoring it like others in the family.

In Chapter 4, I wrote about how our self-concept is shaped by how we think others think of us. And if God calls us a mighty warrior, who are we to argue?! If you doubt your value and your power, reread in many scriptures in God's song about you in Chapter 11. Reread John 3:16. "God is dying to meet you!" Scripture is what we need to base our identity.

And as far Gideon feeling he was the least family member in a family of nobodies? Nope! Just read in Judges 6–7 about his amazing adventure of defeating an army of one-hundred-thousand men with just three hundred other "unimportant" people.

* We get the phrase "putting out a fleece" from Gideon's soggy sheepskin described in Judges 6:36–40.

## PRESCRIPTION

Just last week, I had a college-aged client admit to me, "I'm terrified that I'm going to become my mother." The fear behind this statement was completely valid given that her mother had been physically, verbally, and emotionally abusive to her and her siblings throughout her childhood. Even now, her mother continues to gaslight* and manipulate her along with her family members, causing more distress and hurt. As a college student, she is literally living and experiencing life within Erikson's fifth developmental stage of Identity v. Confusion. So, we'll call her "Erika." She was asking, "Who am I? Who? Who? Who? Who?"

Gil Grissom, the lead *CSI: Crime Scene Investigation* officer at the Las Vegas Police Department, advised his investigators, "Concentrate on what cannot lie: the evidence." In order to solve a major crime in a 42-minute time span on *CSI* or to discover the truth about our identity, we have to look at the evidence. It doesn't lie. Even now, after over twenty years since it aired, I go back to the main premise of *CSI* in my therapy sessions with clients. I often hear these go-to scripts and beliefs: I'm not smart enough. I can't do it. I will fail. I am not as good as they are. I can't handle this. I'm going to be alone forever. It's all my fault. It's all their fault. No one cares. I'm too damaged to be loved. It's not fair. I'm not safe. I'm going to be like my mom. That particular day, I helped Erika look at the evidence of her situation:

Her go-to script told her, "It is hopeless. I'm going to be just like my mom."

☐ **Examine the evidence to see if it is true**
*Nature* says that many mental health issues and addictions are hereditary and do run in families. *Nurture* says that I learn from my environment, so I may have abusive tendencies from what I observed growing up.

☐ **Examine the evidence to see if it is false**
Erica can tell herself: Unlike my mom, I am recognizing my mental health issues and admitting that I need help. Also, unlike my mom,

I am learning new strategies through therapy to manage my emotions and mental health issues. And I am dealing with my past and my trauma so that it doesn't have control over me and I won't repeat the same generational patterns of my family.

☐ **Examine the evidence from God's Word**

There is hope for Erika in Romans 12:2: "Don't copy the behavior and customs of this world, but let God transform you into a new person by changing the way you think. Then you will learn to know God's will for you, which is good and pleasing and perfect."

In therapy and through the work of the Holy Spirit, she can boldly say, I am becoming "A new person. The old life is gone; a new life has begun!" (2 Corinthians 5:17). I don't have to become like my mom.

☐ **Memorize Romans 12:2 and use this four-step process to uncover the evidence of your identity and who you truly are in the eyes of God your Father and Creator**

\* In a 1930s play called *Gas Light* the main character slowly over weeks turns the lights down to convince his wife that the house is not growing darker and darker but that she is going insane.

# 14

# A HEMORRHOID IN THE BODY OF CHRIST

*Some parts of the body [of Christ] that seem weakest and least important are actually the most necessary.*
1 Corinthians 12:22

I often write things that don't allow church members to sit comfortably on their padded pews. So, I joke that, in the Body of Christ, I'm a hemorrhoid.

It's not funny, though, when members with mental health issues of all kinds are treated at church as a pain in the rear.

Henri Nouwen was a renowned author who had taught in divinity schools at Harvard, Notre Dame, and Yale, yet chose to live out the last ten years of his life serving the severely mentally challenged.* He wrote, "In my own community, with many severely handicapped men and women, the greatest source of suffering is not the handicap itself, but the accompanying feelings of being useless, worthless, unappreciated, and unloved."

Apparently, there were people at the First Church of Corinth who were also feeling useless, worthless, unappreciated, and unloved. The apostle Paul writes:

> The body has many different parts, not just one part. If the foot says, "I am not a part of the body because I am not a hand," that does not make it any less a part of the body. And if the ear says, "I am not part of the body because I am not an eye," would that make it any less a

part of the body? If the whole body were an eye, how would you hear? Or if your whole body were an ear, how would you smell anything?

But our bodies have many parts, and God has put each part just where he wants it. How strange a body would be if it had only one part! Yes, there are many parts, but only one body (1 Corinthians 12:14–19)

## I am a part of the Body of Christ

First Paul addresses our view of ourselves. "I'm not a part of the body, because I'm a foot and not a hand."

To make it concrete and current: "I'm not a part of the Church body because I have a disability that limits me to serving donuts, but doesn't allow me to be on the worship team. [Add your own issue about not having a public ministry here.]

But God has a different view of you entirely! "God has put each part just where he wants it." God's kingdom is an upside-down domain! Jesus teaches:

> "Many who are the greatest now will be least important then, and those who seem least important now will be the greatest then" (Matthew 19:30).

> "The greatest among you must be a servant. But those who exalt themselves will be humbled, and those who humble themselves will be exalted" (Matthew 23:11–12).

Donut servers trump worship leaders in God's economy. Upside down!

## I am important in the Body of Christ, regardless of my appearance or behaviors

Paul then addresses other peoples' views of us.

> Some parts of the body that *seem* weakest and least
> important are actually the most necessary. And the parts
> we *regard* as less honorable are those we clothe with the
> greatest care. So we carefully protect those parts that
> should not be seen, while the more honorable parts do
> not require this special care. So God has put the body
> together such that extra honor and care are given to those
> parts that have less dignity. This makes for harmony
> among the members, so that all the members care for
> each other (1 Corinthians 12:20–25, *italics added*).

Paul is honest enough to admit that in the imperfect Church here on earth, some people are deemed "least important," "less honorable," and some are treated with "less dignity." So sad, but so true.

I am appalled by these attitudes in the Church. Jesus certainly lifted up those whom society had pushed down. Women were considered "chattel" or property, children were expendable, and lepers "unclean." And yet the Son of God went out of his way to minister to these and affirm their value.

Remember, we live in a fallen world where the beautiful and talented are worshipped. But in the upside kingdom, even the hemorrhoids in life are "treated with special care." And Downs is up!

* In *The Inner Voice of Love*, Nouwen describes his deep depression: "Everything came crashing down—my self-esteem, my energy to live and work, my sense of being loved, my hope for healing, my trust in God . . . everything. Here I was, a writer about the spiritual life, known as someone who loves God and gives hope to people, flat on the ground and in total darkness." His biographers believe he also struggled with same-sex attraction but never broke his vow of celibacy.

## PRESCRIPTION

Jane had always felt alone and isolated from others her entire life and never thought she was good enough. She felt unseen. As we were talking during a session, she had an idea to send cards and care packages to college students and shut-ins from her church. She figured these people must be feeling alone and unseen as well. Who better to serve them than someone who knows what it's like to feel alone? Jane found her very important part in the body: Card writer and care package sender extraordinaire!

The last ten years of John's anxiety was so overwhelming and debilitating that he had to drop out of college the first week of his freshman year. He was so discouraged that he admitted to me during our first session, "Maybe life isn't worth living." Thankfully he has done a lot of work and is seeing some small wins with his anxiety. He is still extremely anxious, but despite this, he decided to volunteer in the safety and seclusion of the sound booth at church and help with the live-streaming of the church service. John found his very important part in the body: Service streamer and online facilitator exceptional!

Jane and John each found a perfect place to serve despite their traumatic pasts, their mental health struggles, and their feeling unimportant.

☐ **Use your journal to explore: What are my abilities? What do other people affirm about me? How can I use these abilities to build up the Body of Christ?**

Regardless of your physical condition, mental health, or any other factor that you think is keeping you from being important, you can be assured that you have a unique and very important role in the body of Christ. (Dad wrote a book just for those who feel life has passed them by: *If You're Not Dead, You're Not Done! Live with Purpose at Any Age.* You can find free excerpts at agersanonymous.com.)

# 5

# YOU *ARE* ALWAYS ON HIS MIND

*The Lord is thinking about me right now!*
Psalm 40:17 TLB

Aging folk-rocker Willie Nelson's most famous song is "You Were Always on My Mind." In it, he admits he didn't always love his girl-friend, didn't treat her well, made her feel second best, wasn't there when she was lonely, and didn't do the things he should have done. But she is supposed to accept it all because she was always on his mind. No way! She needs to kick this jerk to the curb.

Because it's just a song, we don't have any history of their relation-ship. Maybe she told him to get lost, so this is his way of wooing her back. We don't know. I do know there are many women—and men—who feel they don't deserve someone who will always love them, treat them well, make them feel important, and be there for them in lonely times. You either know one or are one.*

I hope and pray that this section will help you to see that you are important. Despite whatever mental health challenges you are facing, you are worthy of love, respect, and value. And you deserve someone for whom you are always on his/her mind! Yes, those people are often hard to find, but God is literally thinking about you every second! Here are some verses that affirm that:

> "What are people, that you should make so much of us, that you should think of us so often?" (Job 7:17, also Psalms 8:4 and 144:3).

How precious are your thoughts about me, O God. They cannot be numbered! I can't even count them; they outnumber the grains of sand!

And when I wake up, you are still with me! (Psalm 139:17–18).

Let him have all your worries and cares, for he is always thinking about you and watching everything that concerns you (1 Peter 5:7 TLB).

But how can God be thinking of me every second, if he's thinking of you every second? And don't forget, he's thinking every second of eight billion other people. (That's an eight followed by nine zeroes.) A possible answer came with the invention of the supercomputer.

As of November 2021, the Fugaku supercomputer located in Japan is the fastest computer in the world. It is capable of making 442 quadrillion calculations in one second. (That would be 442 followed by *fifteen* zeroes!

Aha! The Japanese computer can make in one second over 53 million calculations for every single person on earth. And the Fugaku computer will probably be obsolete by the time you get to this chapter. So, if a warehouse full of silicon chips can keep track of 442 quadrillion operations per second, it's easy for God to keep track of just eight billion people's every thought every second. And that's just in human terms. Keep in mind, he is eternal which means time means nothing to him! So, in our earthly one second, he can be personally dealing with an unlimited number of people on an infinite list of concerns over an unlimited time period!

So scientifically as well as theologically, God can easily be thinking of me and you every second of every day—and nearly eight billion more!

You are important to God. And you are *always* on his mind!

* If you're in a Willie-Nelson-type relationship, Faith has some helpful posts at recoveringlove.com.

### PRESCRIPTION

I don't know about you, but I am overwhelmed with the thought that all eight billion of us are on his mind every nanosecond, especially little ole me. I was reminded of this just yesterday when I was having dinner with a friend. After hearing me share with her my aching heart about my daughter's emotional and mental struggles with a dating relationship, she recalled, "Actually, a couple of weeks ago, something woke me up in the middle of the night, and your girl came to mind. She was heavy on my heart, and I just couldn't get her off my mind." My friend spent those waking hours in the middle of the night praying fervently for my daughter, weeks before she would even know what was going on in her complicated teenage world at that precise moment that very night.

Clearly that night, my daughter was on God's mind, and he whispered to my friend, "I'm thinking about her, and I want you to join me in that and pray for her right where she is sleeping." I told my daughter about it the next day, and she declared, "Whaaaat? That's really weird but cool!" Yeah, it's over-the-top cool! I like to think about God leaning forward and gazing at us thinking, "Wow. That's my kid. I can't get my precious child off my mind."

Similarly, there have been many nights when God has woken me up and placed someone on my heart to pray for. One of my spiritual gifts is encouragement, so many times when God places something encouraging on my heart to share with someone, I say it. Or I might see some random item at the store or online that makes me think of someone. If I can afford it, I will buy it for them. But if I can't, I will take a picture or screenshot of it and send it to that person with the message, "This made me think of you."

Research shows that doing special things for others gives us a shot of dopamine in our brains and also distracts us for a moment from our own mental and emotional struggles. Thinking of others is like a dose of Prozac for your heart, mind, and soul. Drop a card, a text, or a Facebook private message to let them know that you are thinking about them and praying for them. Write down on your calendar when someone is having surgery or has a big event coming up. On that day, let them know you are thinking of them. If an encouraging thought comes to mind about someone, tell them.

☐ **Let someone know that both God and you are thinking of them today! Let them know they are important and always on God's mind**

# 16

# WHO'S YOUR DADDY?

*For all who are led by the Spirit of God are children of God.*
*So you have not received a spirit that makes you fearful slaves.*
*Instead, you received God's Spirit when he adopted you as his*
*own children. Now we call him, "Abba, Father." For his Spirit*
*joins with our spirit to affirm that we are God's children.*
Romans 8:14–16

"I hate God's guts." Nick had recently started attending the youth group and had wanted to talk after Bible study. One thing I quickly learned as a young youth pastor was that teens always ask a test question. And, then, if you don't totally freak out with the first question, they will ask you their *real* question.

"I'm so sorry. What do you hate about God?" (My eyebrows didn't rise one hair.)

"You've been talking about how God is our heavenly father. Well, if he's my heavenly father, I hate his guts."

"Can you tell me about your earthly father?"

"My old man's a drunken [expletive]. He beats the [expletive] out of my mom, and when he gets bored with that, he beats me. One time, he stripped me naked and threw me out the back door into the snow, and turned the hose on me. I hate his guts." (I was still keeping my cool while thinking *I need to call Child Protective Services as soon as I'm done talking with Nick.*)

It was not hard to understand how Nick could not wrap his head around the idea that God was a father who loved him.

"Oh wow. I am so very sorry. So, who's your favorite TV father?"

"What?"

"Who's your favorite TV father?"

"Uh, I guess Andy Taylor—the sheriff from Mayberry*."

"Yeah, he's a great father. So now, I want you to imagine that God is Andy Taylor times infinity. He loves you infinitely more than you can imagine. In fact, Romans 12:2 says he wants you to have everything that is 'good, pleasing, and perfect.'"

Nick cocked his head and looked serious. "Cool!" And with that, he bounded off to join his friends.

Perhaps you, too, are having a hard time thinking of God as a loving, forgiving, affirming, and nurturing father. Maybe an earthly father has let you down, deserted you, or even abused you physically or sexually.

Despite the image our earthly father has created, Scripture proclaims God loves us more than any TV father.

> "For this is how God loved the world: He gave his one and only Son, so that everyone who believes in him will not perish but have eternal life" (Jesus, John 3:16).

> When we were utterly helpless, Christ came at just the right time and died for us sinners. Now, most people would not be willing to die for an upright person, though someone might perhaps be willing to die for a person who is especially good. But God showed his great love for us by sending Christ to die for us while we were still sinners (Romans 5:6–8).

> I am convinced that nothing can ever separate us from God's love. Neither death nor life, neither angels nor demons, neither our fears for today nor our worries about tomorrow—not even the powers of hell can separate us from God's love. No power in the sky above or in the earth below—indeed, nothing in all creation will ever be able to

separate us from the love of God that is revealed in Christ
Jesus our Lord. (Romans 8:38–39).

Wow! We are loved.

Perhaps your father provided for your every need and never abused
you, but he was cold and distant. You knew he loved you, but he never
came out and overtly said it. God is our Father, but he is so much more
than that. Paul writes in Romans 8:15: "You have not received a spirit
that makes you fearful slaves. Instead, you received God's Spirit when he
adopted you as his own children. Now we call him, 'Abba, Father.'"

First, *abba* was used only by children to address their fathers. So, yes,
it was that child-like address and all the closeness that goes with it. It was
an intimate term. But it also carried the connotation of authority. Abba is
not your playmate—and definitely not your peer! So, if we try to translate
it into modern English it would be more like "King Daddy." I love it! The
all-powerful Creator and All Mighty Ruler of the entire universe gives
his princes and princesses a huge, loving hug and whispers, "I love you."
He's someone that only his children can call by that name. But he's also
someone with power and authority over everyone's very life and breath!

Hail, King Daddy!

## PRESCRIPTION

I am very thankful for the healthy relationship I have with my earthly
daddy and how it has shaped my view of God. I mean, I don't think we
would ever survive the book-writing process together if we didn't have a
healthy relationship. But I know from my years of being a therapist that
there are some pretty terrible dads and moms out there, which makes it
extremely hard to experience and accept God's fatherly love. Cara, whose
father allowed her to be physically and emotionally abused, and then later
abandoned her, was faced with a choice: to forgive or not to forgive. Here
are some steps Cara took to find healing from her past and forgive her
earthly father.

☐ **Do some soul searching and reflection**

Ask, "How is unforgiveness affecting my life and my mental health? How will forgiving this person help me mentally, emotionally, physically, spiritually, and relationally?"

☐ **Pray**

Ask your heavenly father to reveal specific areas of your life where unforgiveness, bitterness, and hate reside, and ask him to show you what to do. Remember that forgiveness is a choice that only you can make.

☐ **Set up a meeting when you are ready**

Consider if it is possible to have a face-to-face conversation with this person. Sometimes the hurt and pain make it impossible to even be in the same room with the one who has wronged us. Or perhaps this person has passed away, is incarcerated, or lives out of state and there is no way to have a healing conversation. This person may still be an unsafe person and meeting in person should not be an option.

A letter is also an option, but it may not always be wise to send it. Whether you send it or not is up to you. Just know that forgiveness is more for you and your mental, emotional, and spiritual healing than it is for the other person.

☐ **If you choose to meet or write a letter, share your feelings openly, honestly, and respectfully**

**Use "I feel" statements** like, "I felt abandoned and hurt when you left me." "You" statements put the person on the defensive. He/she cannot argue with your feelings.

**Communicate that what they did is not okay.** "What you did has negatively affected my life in more ways than you will ever know." Stick to the facts and keep it brief.

**Voice your intentions.** "Despite what has happened, I am choosing to let go of the past and forgive you. I am doing this for me because the anger and bitterness I'm holding onto are perpetuating the hurt and pain in me."

**Set boundaries.** You get to decide how the relationship will proceed. Will there be steps taken towards reconciliation and healing? Is having a long-term relationship with this person healthy for you in the long run? Do you need to make peace in your heart and cut ties? Forgiving someone doesn't mean they have to be a part of your life, especially if they continue to be verbally or emotionally abusive.

**Give them a chance to respond.** Try to put your own emotions aside and truly hear what they have to say. If their response is cold, uncaring, or dismissive, you have the power to end the conversation. "I don't have to continue to be treated this way, I need to end this conversation."

**Thank them for their time and for listening.** Let them know that you appreciate them taking the time to meet with you. Regardless of the outcome, you can walk away from this encounter holding your head high, knowing that you took a huge step in your personal healing!

**Thank your "King Daddy" for forgiving you.** He wants us to walk boldly in his forgiveness, love, and freedom. Say it with me, "Hail, King Daddy!"

'ZAC'
Created 03-02-22
Designer Nathan Watkins
Cheer-leader

V

# I AM PLANNED

*No eye has seen, no ear has heard, and no mind has imagined what God has prepared for those who love him.*

1 Corinthians 2:9

# 17

# "HI, I'M JEREMIAH. MY LIFE ISN'T WORKING OUT AS PLANNED"

*You saw me before I was born. Every day*
*of my life was recorded in your book.*
*Every moment was laid out before a single day had passed.*
Psalm 139:16

Meanwhile, back at the Shalom Support Group, Jeremiah had pulled himself out of his chair with his staff.

"Hi, I'm Jeremiah. My life isn't working out as planned." He pulled a scroll from his pouch. "Here's what I wrote in the first chapter of my book:

"The Lord gave me this message: 'I knew you before I formed you in your mother's womb. Before you were born I set you apart and appointed you as my prophet to the nations. Today I appoint you to stand up against nations and kingdoms' (Jeremiah 1:4-5, 10).

"And, this is ironic, I wrote one of the most popular promises in the whole Bible: 'For I know the plans I have for you, says the Lord. They are plans for good and not for disaster, to give you a future and a hope'" (Jeremiah 29:11).

"Well, it's not worked out like I thought it would! Let's just say, my prophecies are not getting rave reviews. The false prophets have tried to kill me, a Temple official had me beaten and locked in stocks. And I have a terrible case of heartburn trying to keep my message to myself (Jeremiah 20:9).

Instead of a revered prophet, I'm known as the 'weeping prophet.' Nope. Not what I signed up for!"

A show of hands, please. How many of you are living a life you never signed up for? Yes, I see that hand. And another. Me too. But Scripture gives me a sense of confidence that my life is not just one of chance, accident, or even karma.

## I was planned

Remember that you are fearfully and wonderfully made! Theologians love to argue about just how much of who we are is God-created or genetically determined. Was it God or a fallen world that is responsible for your mental health or developmental challenge? I have a degree in theology, and I can assure you without a single doubt . . . I have no clue.* But no matter how your cards were dealt, the game is rigged by God himself. He is able to take our situation and redeem it for his glory. For instance:

> As Jesus was walking along, he saw a man who had been blind from birth. "Rabbi," his disciples asked him, "why was this man born blind? Was it because of his own sins or his parents' sins?"
>
> "It was not because of his sins or his parents' sins," Jesus answered. "This happened so the power of God could be seen in him" (John 9:1–3).

Certain sexually-transmitted diseases can cause blindness in babies who are infected during natural delivery. So, the disciples were asking who was sexually promiscuous: the blind man or his parents? Jesus answered with an emphatic neither! "This happened so the power of God could be seen in him."

I believe that it is the result of both God and genetics! It's in the same

I-don't-understand category of God being three and one, that Jesus is 100 percent God and 100 percent human, and that I have freewill but God's desires *will* be accomplished!

So rather than wrestling with the questions, I try to focus on how I can glorify God with my challenges. As you'll read in chapter twenty-one, I give God the credit for any writing or speaking success this ADD-addled, clinically-depressed introvert has obtained. It gives him glory and at the same time keeps me humble in any praise for my accomplishments.

## My days are planned

Even more amazing—and mysterious—is the claim, translated in the *New Living Translation*, that "Every day of my life was recorded in your book. Every moment was laid out before a single day had passed" (Psalm 139:16).

Other versions give the impression that all the days of *fetal development* were recorded and carried out until birth:

> You could see my body grow each passing day. You listed all my parts, and not one of them was missing (*Easy-to-Read Version*).
>
> Thine eyes did see my substance yet being imperfect; and in thy book all my members were written, which were then formed, without lacking one of them (*Jubilee Bible 2000*).

However, most Bible translators leave us with a baffling mystery!

> All my days were written in your book and planned before a single one of them began (*Christian Standard Bible*).

> Even before I was born, you had written in your book everything I would do (*Contemporary English Bible*).

Every detail of my life was already written in Your book; You established the length of my life before I ever tasted the sweetness of it (*The Voice*).

But how can God plan out every single day of my life? How can he know the exact time and date of my death? I'll have to file that in the I-don't-understand category! I can't make sense of it, but it makes sense of my life.

As we'll share in the next chapter, we are fearfully and wonderfully made. And our life as well is just as fearfully and wonderfully planned!

* I've written a book that honestly looks at the why questions of Christianity: *God I Don't Understand: Struggling with Unanswered Prayer, Unfulfilled Promises, Unpunished Evil.* Yeah, I hate this shameless self-promotion, but people who have read it found it very helpful. You can read excerpts at: www.jameswatkins.com/idontunderstand (And now back to our regularly scheduled chapter.)

## PRESCRIPTION

"Why" is a question we often ask ourselves. In those dark days during my divorce, I was training for my first half marathon and running alone on those country roads, I would literally scream out loud to God, "Why did you do this to me? Why is this happening? What did I do wrong?"

Be honest with God and don't be afraid to ask him "why?" Writing down the questions is like pinning butterflies to a display board. Otherwise, those queries flutter free in the meadows of our minds. So, "pin" them down in your journal so you can examine them and deal effectively with them.

God knew all these things would happen, and we can know that he works all things for our good and that we are a part of his glory story.

☐ **Write out your "why" questions in your journal. Be brutally honest. He's not going to be offended in the least. In fact, he will appreciate your intimacy with him!**

# 18

# I AM FEARFULLY AND WONDERFULLY MADE

*For you created my inmost being; you knit me together*
*in my mother's womb. I praise you because*
*I am fearfully and wonderfully made.*
*My frame was not hidden from you when I was made in the secret*
*place, when I was woven together in the depths of the earth.*
Psalm 139:13, 15 NIV


When King David penned Psalm 139, he used two powerful words to describe just how "fearfully" and "wonderfully" we are made.

The Hebrew word for fearfully is *yârê'*. (Don't worry, that won't be on the test.) It means to stand in awe, to be astonished, to reverence, to honor, and to respect. (In full disclosure, it can also refer to fear, horror, and terror—the emotions produced by looking in the mirror the first thing in the morning.*)

David uses the word *pâlâh* rendered in English as wonderfully. (Again, not on the test.) But it goes much further than just your mom saying of your Sunday school craft for Mother's Day, "Isn't that wonderful?" Which is her kind way of saying, "Great. Another piece of junk to dust." No, the Hebrew word means to be distinct, marked out, separated, distinguished, marvelous, and to be truly wonderful.

I distinctly remember my Freshman Biology professor droning on about the evolution of the human body and all the time thinking, *I don't have enough faith to be an evolutionist.* I doubt it was his intention, but my faith and awe of an Intelligent Designer increased the more he talked about how intricate parts of the body—especially the brain—were accidental mutations that helped the simple cells survive and evolve into a university professor.

We now know that Charles Darwin's "simple cell," from which all life supposedly evolved, actually contains enough genetic information to fill a printout the size of the *Encyclopedia Britannica*. That's just one cell! Our brains are made of billions of nerve cells that communicate through trillions of connections called synapses.

Here are some more amazing facts about the three-pound miracle between your ears!

First, the human brain is the world's smallest, yet most powerful supercomputer using only ten watts of electricity. The Fugaku supercomputer I wrote about in Chapter 15 takes up nearly two tennis counts of space and uses nearly thirty million watts of energy. Since the body generates its own power, it has no operating expenses. Well, except for food, but nothing like the three hundred thousand dollars per hour to run the supercomputer.

Second, the human brain has the advantage over the supercomputer in the number of processing units. One central processing unit (CPU) makes up a "node." The Fugaku supercomputer is made up of 158,976 nodes! A brain contains 86 billion neurons, with each forming connections to other neurons adding up to a quadrillion connections. (A quadrillion is one-thousand trillion!) During our lifetime these neurons can combine, increasing storage capacity. And contrary to the claim we use only 10 percent of our brain, neuroscientists have found all our brain is active all the time—even busier while we're sleeping!

Third, while over five hundred miles of fiber optic cable in the supercomputer can send information at the speed of light, our brain's signals at 268 miles per hour can still reach any part of our body in less than one-millionth of a second.

And fourth, the human brain beats the supercomputer in costs. While humans cost nothing to create, admittedly it does cost an estimated $267,000 to raise a child to eighteen years of age. But that's comparatively little to Fugaku's billion-dollar-plus price tag.

We are fearfully and wonderfully made—and that's just the top of our heads. It would take several volumes to cover the other 90 percent of our bodies.

So, no matter how severe our mental health challenges may be, the mere fact that I'm writing and you're reading this book is a powerful testament to the incredible work of God we are. Stand in awe, be astonished, reverence, honor, and respect who he has created. You are distinct, marked out, separated, distinguished, marvelous, and truly wonderful.

* If an old-looking person stares back at you from the mirror, you'll enjoy my hopeful and humorous devotional book *If You're Not Dead, You're Not Done!* It teaches ten characteristics that will fill your Social Security years with purpose, passion, and pizazz. A perfect gift for birthdays, retirements, and hip replacement rehab.

## PRESCRIPTION

I remember the awe and the surrealness when I gave birth to my first child. As I was lying there in the delivery room, holding my little miracle, I fully realized that this was the creature who invaded my body and was causing my nightly heartburn, making my stomach move and roll like a wave, and jamming its feet into my ribs twenty-four/seven. Obviously, I knew that I was pregnant and a baby was growing inside of me, but seeing her face to face was when I officially realized that this little human was what lived inside of my body for nine months!

Now that my girls are teenagers, I am in awe at the fact that these girls who are taller than me, once fit inside of my body. Our bodies are truly a miracle that could only be created by a loving, thoughtful, and intentional God for all of our parts to work together in such an intricate way.

Let's take a few moments to sit in awe of our bodies. And it involves chocolate!

☐ **Enjoy a delicious piece of chocolate!**

Take a bite of your favorite chocolate bar. Slowly savor each bite. Feel the texture as it goes into your mouth. What tastes and sensations do you feel in your mouth? Is it smooth or crunchy? Is it sweet or salty? Is your mouth watering? What else do you notice? Think about how your brain and tastebuds work together to fully experience the pleasure of eating chocolate.

Do you have a feeling of happiness or relaxation? Take some time to notice what is going on in your mouth and the rest of your body. I am in awe of the way Dove dark chocolate calms my body and takes the stress of the day away for a moment.

☐ **In your journal, write down ways in which you are fearfully and wonderfully made: physically, mentally, and socially. Be in awe of the wonder that is you!**

Think of other ways to bring more awareness to your body and the fearfully and wonderfully made creation that it is. Regardless of your current mental or physical status, you can stand in awe of your body and how God created it to work. Walk or sit with your head a little higher today because you are "fearfully and wonderfully made."

# 19

# YES, I *AM* A PIECE OF WORK!

*Thank you for making me so wonderfully complex!*
*Your workmanship is marvelous—how well I know it.*
Psalm 139:14

The trash-talk term "piece of work" was actually a high compliment from William Shakespeare's play "Hamlet."

As you may remember from English Literature, the king of Denmark has been murdered and his wife, Queen Gertrude, has married his brother, Claudius. The king's son, Hamlet, is visited by the dead king's ghost who warns him that Mom's new husband killed Dad. Hamlet vows revenge! And like most Shakespeare plays, by the final curtain, most of the cast is dead including the deeply depressed and suicidal Hamlet and the murderous, power-hungry Claudius. So, here's how Shakespeare* created the phrase:

> What a piece of work is man! How noble in reason!
> how infinite in faculties! in form and moving, how express
> and admirable! in action how like an angel! in apprehen-
> sion, how like a god! the beauty of the world! the paragon
> of animals!

According to Grammatist.com, around the turn of the twentieth century, the glowing compliment mutated into a term that meant "someone hard to deal with or of low character in the phrase a nasty piece of work."

It immigrated across the pond, and in the 1970s evolved into "a real piece of work."

Actually, the concept goes back to the time of another king, David (Psalm 139:14).

> For we are God's masterpiece. He has created us anew
> in Christ Jesus, so we can do the good things he planned
> for us long ago (Ephesians 2:10).

> And I am certain that God, who began the good work
> within you, will continue his work until it is finally finished
> on the day when Christ Jesus returns (Philippians 1:6).

So, yes, we *are* a piece of work: God's work! We are God's masterpiece! He has created us anew in Christ Jesus, so we can do the good things he planned for us long ago.

And, we are a piece of God's work in progress! He will "continue his work until it is finally finished on the day when Christ Jesus returns" (Philippians 1:9).

Lysa TerKeurst wrote on her Facebook page: "We are a glorious work of God in progress. We are imperfect because we are unfinished." (Ooh, that's good! Underline that! Put a star on the outside margin!)

And every single piece of our experience is working toward his finished product!

"We know that God causes everything to work together for the good of those who love God and are called according to his purpose . . . to become like his Son" (Romans 8:28-29).

Several years ago, I made a lute—those ancient guitars with the gourd-shaped bodies—out of walnut. I'm sure the walnut tree, we'll call him Wally, was not happy when he was cut down, sawed up, planed smooth, and then sculpted, chiseled, and sanded. We all have those kinds of painful experiences, not just in ordinary life, but particularly in the life of one with mental health issues.

But now Wally is out of the rain and snow, summer heat, and safe from woodpeckers! He sits comfortably and proudly on display in our entertainment center.

And soon we too will be proudly displayed by our Creator:

"He chose to give birth to us by giving us his true word. And we, out of all creation, became his prized possession" (James 1:18).

So, yes. I am a piece of work!

\* While William Shakespeare died over 400 years ago, his original phrases are still used today: It's Greek to me, eaten out of house and home, neither rhyme nor reason, too much of a good thing, I have not slept one wink, all that glitters isn't gold, brave new world, wild-goose chase, and many more.

## PRESCRIPTION

Yes, my dad is definitely a piece of work. But so am I, and so are all of you!

When I think about the fact that we are God's masterpieces, I am reminded of those days long ago when my girls would bring home art projects from school or give me special homemade gifts for Mother's Day. Granted these were not at all close to being worthy of having a place of honor at the Louvre in Paris or in a traveling art exhibit making its way into art museums across the country. But these might as well be because, for me, these were beautiful works of art created by the minds, hands, and hearts of my children. As far as I was concerned, these were masterpieces.

Think about the last piece of art or homemade gifts that your child or someone else's child made for you. You may have had no idea what the drawing was or the mess that was on the paper. But it didn't matter. It was the most beautiful and precious unidentified object that you had ever seen. No doubt, your face beamed with pleasure as you oohed and ahhed over their artwork.

When we see ourselves as a blockhead, God sees a beautiful wooden sculpture. When you feel like a piece of dirt, God sees you as a unique individual he created from dust. When you feel like a worthless lump lay-ing on the couch all day, God sees a useful piece of pottery that he created for a purpose.

Even more, think about the last time you made something and stood back in awe of what you put your mind to and created. I can think of a few birthday cakes I made and thought, *Wow, I should sign up for* Cupcake Wars, Sugar Rush, *or at least* Nailed It.

I've also done some outdoor projects that have looked like something out of *Better Homes and Gardens*, and I just stand back and admire how amazing it turned out. I just can't stop looking at it and thinking to myself, *Wow. I did that!*

What are some projects that you have created that make you think, *Wow, I did that!* Whatever it is, you can stand back from your accomplish-ments filled with pride and a sense of accomplishment.

Next time your child brings home a piece of art or a homemade gift, or you do something around your house that makes you feel good about yourself and you can't stop admiring it, think about how your heavenly Father looks at you, his beautiful creation. You are his special treasure, a masterpiece.

☐ **Use your journal to write down things God appreciates about you. Write down what the Bible says. Then write down what you think is specific to you. Don't be bashful to write just how much there is about you for him to appreciate! (Be honest! You're so much better than you think!)**

# 20

# A GOOD, PLEASING, AND PERFECT PLAN

*Don't copy the behavior and customs of this world, but let God
transform you into a new person by changing the way you think.
Then you will learn to know God's will for you, which is
good and pleasing and perfect.*
Romans 12:2

My dad had mad mechanical skills. He could keep our old Chevy running by changing spark plugs, distributors, brakes—whatchamacallits—well into the late seventies. He and his *Chilton Repair Manual for 1957 Chevrolets could fix it.*

Even though I was his scrub nurse handing him tools for major replacement operations—"Three-eighth-inch wrench" "Half-inch socket" "Thingamajig"—internal combustion engines and I never became good friends.

Fast forward fifteen years. While on a mission trip, I was assigned to drive a large dump truck to collect the brush we were clearing for a building on the campus. After several trips back and forth between the clearing and the dump area, I noticed I was running low on fuel. I had noticed a large gas tank, between locations so—trying to be helpful—I stopped and filled up the tank. I drove off, but only got about fifty yards before the truck coughed, sputtered, and died on the gravel road. The mission director came by a bit later.

"What happened?"

"I don't know. It can't be out of gas, because I just filled it up."

"Uh . . . Where did you fill it up?"

"That gas tank just down the road."

I could tell by his expression, he was trying his best not to say something un-missionary-like.

"That was a *gasoline* tank."

"Yeah," I innocently—and ignorantly—replied.

"This is a *diesel* truck!"

It took us an hour to empty out the tank and then refill it with the proper fuel.

I had such good intentions, but the dump truck was never designed for gasoline. We often run into the same problem in our lives. We want to have a great life, but we're not following the owner's manual, so things are not running well.

We think we know best how to run our lives, but there's a trail of crashed and burned relationships, wrecked health, and broken dreams littering the road behind us. I hope you discovered in Section III just how much God loves you. You are his beloved Creation, and because of that love, he has given instructions for a "good, pleasing, and perfect" plan. And when we don't follow them, our lives run as well as that dump truck with the wrong fuel. Our physical, social, mental, or sexual life can end up in the junkyard without following God's commandments.

The majority of our culture may believe the prescribed oil types, kinds of alternators, fuel filters, gaps of spark plugs—even windshield wiper types—are rigid, arbitrary, intolerant, out of date, and even hateful. Doesn't matter. Your vehicle and your life are going to run smoother only if you follow the manual.*

So, here are some promises from the instruction manual:

> Study this Book of Instruction continually. Meditate
> on it day and night so you will be sure to obey everything
> written in it. Only then will you prosper and succeed in all
> you do (Joshua 1:8).

> But if you look carefully into the perfect law that sets
> you free, and if you do what it says and don't forget what
> you heard, then God will bless you for doing it (James 1:25).

Once the mission director got over the shock that I wasted a whole tank of gas and took an hour out of his busy schedule, he was gracious, forgiving, and even thanked me for my work. And unlike roadside assistance that only shows up in times of trouble, God wants to travel with us on this road trip of life. He even brings snacks called blessings.

* Please notice that it is God's plan that is "good, pleasing, and perfect." Because we live in a broken world where even creation has been damaged by the Fall (Romans 8:22-23), life itself is not always good, pleasing, or perfect. But God can redeem each situation for our good (Romans 8:28) if—and only if—we will follow his instruction manual.

## PRESCRIPTION

Unfortunately, I know this scenario all too well. Except it wasn't me pouring gas into a diesel engine, but pouring less than God's best into my heart—and it was tearing the engine of my soul apart. After my divorce, I was wounded more than I knew. And I didn't want to feel the intense emotional pain anymore. My heart needed a hit of something to find relief from the pain I was feeling deep in my soul. And so, I set out to fill my heart with whatever it wanted. And I looked for love and acceptance in all the wrong places: in the arms of men and desperately searching for my happily ever after.

I was living a double life by going to church and acting like the perfect Christian. It looked like I had it all together, but my sin was controlling me and eating my soul. It was the most miserable and anxious couple of years I've ever experienced. But unlike being betrayed by my ex, I was doing this harm to myself.

A few years into riding this roller coaster with my head spinning and feeling nauseous, I was driving to work, consumed with anxiety and a spiritual war within me. Almost audibly, as if through my car stereo, I heard God whisper so lovingly to my heart, "I made you for more than this." He lovingly urged me to be obedient, not for his good, but for my own. He wanted so much more for me and to experience his good, pleasing, and perfect plan. He pleaded longingly, "I can't give you the desires of your heart if you are clinging to these relationships and behaviors that are causing your misery."

Miles and miles from where I needed to be, my Abba father left the ninety-nine to rescue me. He filled me with a desire to know, believe, and follow his good, pleasing, and perfect plan for me.

☐ **What behaviors am I doing that are not good, pleasing, or perfect for me?**

☐ **How might things look different for me if I did what God was asking me to do?**

☐ **What specific steps do I need to take to begin to surrender to him and his good, pleasing, and perfect plan for me?**

# VI

# I AM FORGIVEN

*For he has rescued us from the kingdom of darkness and transferred us into the Kingdom of his dear Son, who purchased our freedom and forgave our sins.*

Colossians 1:13-14

# 21

# "HI, I'M RAHAB.
# I RUN AN *INN*"

*If we claim we have no sin, we are only fooling ourselves
and not living in the truth. But if we confess our sins to him,
he is faithful and just to forgive us our sins and
to cleanse us from all wickedness.*
1 John 1:8

"Who would like to start our sharing today?"
The woman in the red robe had joined the Shalom Support
Group a few weeks ago but had always sat alone and had never spoken.

"Uh . . . Hi . . . I'm . . . uh . . . Rahab of Jericho and I ran a very
popular . . ." She stopped abruptly, then made "air quotes" with her fin-
gers as she bowed her head and voiced "inn." Everyone instantly under-
stood her meaning. The kind of inn with hourly rates and an exclusively
male clientele.

"One day some nice Jewish boys came by and seemed very nervous
and uncomfortable. Well, of course, they would be knowing the kind of
inn I ran. But they weren't worried about breaking their God's commandments or the wrath of their godly mothers. No, they were spying out the
city for an invasion. Anyway, they promised my family and I would be
saved if I hid them. I just needed to hang a scarlet cord out the window to
be spared during the attack. They saved my life and my family's.

"But now I'm so conflicted. I chose to follow their God, but my
past is following me."

If we're more than one minute old, we have a past. (Okay, it's only sixty seconds, but it *is* a past.)

While I'm now an author who has written three books on sexual purity and seventeen more on living a holy life, that was never my intention. Nope! I was planning to write porn. It's much more lucrative and, for a junior high boy, something I was very interested in exploring. So, while I had a squeaky-clean demeanor with perfect attendance in Sunday school, I had a mind filled with vile and perverted smut.

And add to that depression and anxiety along with suicidal ideations, my mind was a very dark, dank place.

## I'm a mess

So, at a large conference, I shared that this "award-winning author" and "globe-trotting speaker" is just one great, big, slobbering *mess*.

I mentioned my alphabet of mental health challenges and coming across as an energetic and enthusiastic speaker when people and conferences drain my emotional batteries. I'd much rather be alone in my home office rather than speaking to an auditorium full of strangers. I really do love people. I wouldn't keep putting myself in unfamiliar situations with unknown people if I didn't! But people wear out this introvert.

And so, this outgoing, outspoken, outrageous author/speaker is, in reality, an Oscar-worthy actor who feels introverted, inadequate, and very insecure.

So, I asked the people in the audience to turn to the person on their right and say, "I'm a mess." Then, I asked them to turn to the person on their left and say, "You're a mess."

After the keynote, a woman came up to me in tears and gave me a hug. More like a bear hug. No, a grizzly bear[*] hug, and sobbed, "I'm so glad someone besides me is a mess."

It is liberating to realize, "I'm a mess. You're a mess." In fact, that should come as no surprise.

For everyone has sinned; we all fall short of God's glorious standard (Romans 3:23).

The temptations in your life are no different from what others experience (1 Corinthians 10:13).

"Healthy people don't need a doctor—sick people do. I have come to call not those who think they are righteous, but those who know they are sinners" (Jesus, Mark 2:17).

But here's the wonderful mess-age for all of us messes:

## We have a Mess-iah!

Just look at the hot messes that God has chosen to use: Moses wasn't a speaker. Gideon was the least of his tribe. David was a shepherd boy when he squared off against the giant Goliath. Daniel was a POW. Jeremiah was depressed with suicidal ideations. Peter had a severe case of "hoof-in-mouth" disease. James and John were hotheads nicknamed "Sons of Thunder." The woman at the well was the original "Desperate Housewife." Paul had a "thorn in the flesh." Mark was a quitter. Timothy was timid and sickly.

So, be encouraged and repeat after me, "I'm a mess. You're a mess." And then proudly proclaim, "That's why we have a Messiah."

\* Unlike black bears, grizzlies have a shoulder hump, smaller ears, and much larger claws. Personally, I don't want to get close enough to notice those differences!

## PRESCRIPTION

Heather, the survivor of sexual assault by a family member, sits on my couch week after week and discloses some of the most awful, heart-wrenching things I have heard in my almost seventeen years of doing therapy. And yet she still hasn't even been able to utter the worst of the details that are still haunting her heart, mind, body, and soul. Immobilizing fear of even letting these terrible traumatic secrets out into the light grips her. Just the recent stories she has told of someone breaking into her home, tampering with her vehicle, and even evidence of someone stalking her all because she is planning to testify, are enough to feel like a *Dateline* episode. But this real life, it's her life.

Week after week, update after update, she shares these unthinkable events and circumstances, and then ends her story matter of factly with, "But I'm fine." She smirks knowing what my response will be, "No you aren't." As odd as it sounds, this has become her standard response, and to us, it's become like a little comedy bit or inside joke between us. She has begun opening up more about the fact that she is in fact not fine, and is in all actuality, a total hot mess inside. She knows it. I know it. We're all a mess!

☐ **Make a list of ways you feel like a hot mess**

What is causing my depression or anxiety?

What thoughts or memories seem to repeat constantly in my mind?

What addiction has its grip on me?

What family situation is causing me so much distress?

☐ **Give your mess to the Messiah**

Tuck this list in your Bible, tie it to a helium balloon and let it go or just hold it in your hands as if you are lifting it to him. It's time to stand up and exclaim, "My life and my mental health may be a mess, but my hope is in the Messiah!"

# 22

# I AM MADE BRAND NEW

*Anyone who belongs to Christ has become a new person.*
*The old life is gone; a new life has begun!*
2 Corinthians 5:17

While I was serving as campus pastor at a Christian university, Darla dropped by my office, slumped in the chair in front of my desk, and sighed, "I'm worthless."

"I'm so sorry, Darla. Why do you think that?"

She told me—in graphic detail—about a lifetime of being raped by both her father and her two brothers.

"I'm worthless. No one is going to want me as a dirty, used piece of meat."

I tried to maintain my poker-faced, objective "counselor" face, but all I could say is, "I am so very, very sorry, Darla. So very sorry."

After seven years of abuse, Darla had gone to her school counselor. She had been placed in a Christian foster home where she had asked Jesus into her life. Although Christ does make us "new creations" instantly, it often takes months or years for us to view ourselves as brand new.

As we talked almost weekly for the next six months, I discovered a girl who felt betrayed, abandoned, alone, unable to trust any kind of authority, confused about self-identity, violated, disrespected, used, dirty, trapped, robbed, guilty, responsible for the evil acts beyond her control, full of love-hate feelings toward her family, and depressed. (Post-Traumatic Stress Disorder was not widely recognized at the time, but she had all the symptoms in today's *DSM* checklist.)

Your regrets may not be as dramatic, but I imagine there are things you did—perhaps because of your mental health issues—for which you now feel ashamed. I know my ADD caused me to impulsively do all kinds of embarrassing things that my lawyer says I can't talk about. Ha! (Fortunately, no facial tattoos. Whew!) But here's the good news:

## A relationship with God dramatically changes a person

The church in Corinth* was filled with Christians who had been involved in all kinds of immoral behavior before coming to Christ. The apostle Paul lists "those who indulge in sexual sin, or who worship idols, or commit adultery, or are male prostitutes, or practice homosexuality, or are thieves, or greedy people, or drunkards, or are abusive, or cheat people" (1 Corinthians 6:9-10).

But he continues to write, "Some of you were once like that. But you *were cleansed*; you were *made holy*; you were *made right with God* by calling on the name of the Lord Jesus Christ and by the Spirit of our God" (6:11, *italics added*).

## A relationship with God makes a person brand-new

In John 3:16, Jesus declares that when we invite him into our lives, we start life over! We are born again! Regardless of our past and behavior, we are innocent as newborn babies in God's eyes.

Unfortunately, we can't deliberately forget the way God can. But he has provided a way that we can experience mental healing as well.

## A relationship with God makes a person's mind brand-new

As Darla and I talked over the next few months, she began to see herself as this "brand-new person." One week she shared two scriptures that had encouraged her that mental healing was possible:

> Instead, let the Spirit renew your thoughts and attitudes. Put on your new nature, created to be like God— truly righteous and holy (Ephesians 4:23–24).

Don't copy the behavior and customs of this world, but let God transform you into a new person by changing the way you think. Then you will learn to know God's will for you, which is good and pleasing and perfect (Romans 12:2).

Darla's freedom from her past, however, wasn't easy.

## A relationship with God doesn't change everything

Unfortunately, some things do not change because we ask forgiveness for our past and totally commit our lives to God. Legal, social, and natural consequences do not change. Innocence in God's eyes—and our own—doesn't change our earthly reputation. And—this is important—the people who hurt you probably won't change. So, if you are in a physically or mentally abusive relationship, get out *now*. Their apologies and promises to change are manipulative lies unless they take deliberate action to get help and change.

It has taken a lot of time, prayer, and professional counseling, but today Darla has learned to overcome her past. She's learned to forgive her father and brothers. She's now happily married with grown children and is working as a therapist to troubled students. God can do the same for you and your friends!

* The ancient city of Corinth was named after Corinthus, who may or may not have been a son of Zeus. It was rumored he was rather the son of Marathon. Little is known of Marathon and Corinthus as they were not revered in the pantheon of gods. I suspect that Marathon is now the god of Big Oil, while Corinthus rules over gas station hotdogs.

## PRESCRIPTION

As I read Darla's story, I thought I was reading about my friend, Cara. We first met a little over a year ago when I volunteered at a local halfway house for those in recovery from addiction. She was broken by sexual abuse as a child and grew up in foster homes. She had a long history of toxic and abusive relationships and had just gotten out of jail for possession of methamphetamine. She was definitely the poster child for being a hot mess.

Thankfully, Cara is definitely *not* that person anymore. Since I first met her, she has accepted Jesus as her Savior, she was baptized and even asked me to be her spiritual mentor. She is coming up on two years clean and looking at her and the life she has built, you would never in a million years imagine that she was at rock bottom with absolutely nothing not long ago. I am honored and privileged to have a front-row seat to the miraculous transformation in her life.

What's your story?

☐ **Start by meditating on Romans 12:2 and then answer the following questions**:

Where am I today in the transformation process?

What might be some thoughts or behaviors God is wanting me to give up or change?

What would it look like for you to let God transform you?

☐ **If you have experienced this kind of transformation yourself, take time today to thank him for the change**

☐ **Reflect on what is new about you today and where you have come from. Share with someone what he has done in you, and then shout from the mountaintops, "I am made new!"** And write these in your journal.

# 23

# I AM FORGIVEN—BY *ME*

*I focus on this one thing: Forgetting the past and*
*looking forward to what lies ahead.*
Philippians 3:13

If you're like me—and I sincerely hope you're not—your mental health issues have left you with regrets for things you've done in the past. For instance, my ADD has compelled me to do all kinds of disastrous and at times dangerous things! As a kid, I attempted to make rocket fuel with everything I found in the garage marked "Flammable." I took clocks, radios, and other small appliances apart to see how they worked. And, of course, couldn't put them back together!

Whether humorous or horrific, innocent or felonious, we have all done things we are now ashamed of. And we may be having a hard time forgiving ourselves. Our inner critic calls us stupid, irresponsible, weak, and . . . well, you know the accusations.

But here's what our Creator promises:

> But if we confess our sins to him, he is faithful and just to forgive us our sins and to cleanse us from all wickedness (1 John 1:9).

> Then he says, "I will never again remember their sins and lawless deeds" (Hebrews 10:17).

He has removed our sins as far from us as the east is
from the west (Psalm 103:12).

Yes, we've all done horrible things, but God the Father has forgiven us
through the death of his Son for the punishment of our sins.* He will never
again remember our sins and will remove guilt as far as the east is from the
west. We should do the same.

* Jeffrey Dahmer (1960–1994) was a serial killer, rapist, and canni-
bal who killed at least seventeen young men and ate perhaps ten of them.
Following "The Milwaukee Monster's" arrest and imprisonment, he became
a born-again Christian—forgiven of all his sins. That is *amazing* grace!

## PRESCRIPTION

After surviving the difficult season of going through a divorce and
beginning a journey alone, I happened to find running as a helpful outlet and
started training for my first half-marathon. I specifically remember during
my first race around mile three, I was taken aback when I was passed by
a firefighter dressed in full firefighting gear. He and his firehouse buddies
were running the 13.1 miles donning their coats, pants, boots, helmets, and
even their oxygen tanks! That's approximately forty-five extra pounds,
and can you believe that they passed me? Talk about a sense of shame.

But when I think about the guilt and shame that we hold onto and
carry throughout our lives, I think about what it must have been like to
run on that 75-degree day, covered from head to toe in forty-five pounds
of extra weight. Guilt and shame are some of the most immobilizing,
heavy, and destructive emotions we can have and hold. They hold us
captive in the past so that we dwell on the past and what we have done,
all the while our negative thoughts about ourselves snowball and keep us
from fully enjoying life and walking in freedom from our past grow and
ever-increase.

## ☐ Let it go

Sometimes, we hold on to guilt and shame for things that aren't even ours to hold onto, and we live our lives beating ourselves up for something that isn't even ours to carry. If you discover that what you've been carrying and holding onto isn't yours to carry and in reality, you have no responsibility for it, lay it all down. Right now. Leave all that gear wherever you are in your race, and run towards the finish line in freedom.

## ☐ Take responsibility and confess your wrongs

Guilt and shame tell us to hide and not let anyone know what we've done. Alcoholics Anonymous (AA) teaches, "We are only as sick as our secrets." We will continue to suffer at the hands of guilt and shame if we keep our secrets locked up inside. Reach out to someone whom you trust and take the first step in forgiving yourself by shedding light on what has been hiding and lurking in the depths of your soul. Acknowledge and own up to the facts of what you did both to yourself and to the person you have wronged.

## ☐ Apologize and make amends for your behavior

We can't go back and change what we've done, but we can take responsibility for it and admit our wrongs to the person we hurt or admit what we have done. We can say we are sorry and ask if there's anything we can do to make it right. Sometimes it's not possible to make amends because it may cause more harm or that person is not available, not willing, or has passed away. Regardless, we must make amends in whatever way possible.

## ☐ Commit to avoiding the same mistakes in the future

Set specific goals to make changes in your behavior. Maybe it means joining a self-help group, going to therapy, or simply committing to make a different choice the next time.

In my addiction treatment programs, I have clients make a "Relapse Prevention Plan." It is a detailed plan of how they will do things differently to continue in the change process and what they plan to do in every area of their lives to support their recovery and prevent them from going back to who they were before.

## ☐ Don't aim for perfection; aim for progress

Know that life is a learning process, and we can always learn from our mistakes. We aren't going to be perfect on this side of heaven.

So, join me in letting him remove our sins and stripping off the heavy fire gear of guilt and shame, and run with me, free from the weightiness of the past. And even if you pass me, I'll be cheering you on!

# 24

# LOVING YOURSELF
# AS YOUR NEIGHBOR

*"Love your neighbor as yourself."*
Leviticus 19:18, Matthew 22:26

When Jesus was asked what was the greatest commandment, he answered:

> "'You must love the Lord your God with all your heart, all your soul, and all your mind.' This is the first and greatest commandment. A second is equally important: 'Love your neighbor as yourself.' The entire law and all the demands of the prophets are based on these two commandments" (Matthew 22:37–40).

I hope Jesus doesn't object, but I'd like to add a third commandment: *Love yourself as your neighbor.* Let me explain before you recruit an angry mob with torches and pitchforks to burn me at the stake for heresy.

Here's my point: Do you treat yourself as well as you treat your neighbor? Are you patient with yourself? Can you forgive yourself? Are you merciful, kind, gentle, and patient with yourself? Do you encourage yourself, or do you use abusive language in your self-talk? And are you building yourself up in the Lord?

I would never say the things I say to myself to my neighbor. First, he's a big, muscular guy who would probably pound me into the ground like a tent peg! And second, that is no way to talk to a beloved creation of God, mental health issues and all.

It's hard enough carrying the cross of anxiety, bipolar, depression, panic attacks, PTSD, schizophrenia, or—feel free to add your own issue—without piling on self-loathing!

Before I was diagnosed and properly medicated for clinical depression, I would try to talk myself out of bed with all the bravado of a drill sergeant.

"Watkins! Get out of that [bleeping] bed, soldier. You're a disgrace to the uniform, so get that lazy, good-for-nothin' [bleeping] sack of [bleep] you call a soldier on its feet! Do you hear me, Watkins?!"

And on and on Sergeant Watkins would scream in my face with his nose almost touching mine. To which I'd simply react by burrowing deeper under the covers and the pity pit I had dug for myself. Needless to say, Sergeant Watkins' inspiring motivational talks* were not helpful.

Yes, as people with mental health issues, we make a lot of road trips to the Land of Bad Decisions, but some are totally out of our control. We need to extend grace to ourselves. So, if God has forgiven us, who are we to think we have more judicial power than the Lord Almighty! (That's good. You may want to underline it and put a big ! in the margin.) Forgiveness often has progress and setbacks. So, treat yourself as you treat your neighbor.

* Fear and love are considered the two most powerful motivators. The apostle Paul addresses these instigators: "For God has not given us a spirit of fear and timidity, but of power, love, and self-discipline" (2 Timothy 1:7). Yes, two thousand years later, studies have shown love is the most effective motivator!

## PRESCRIPTION

Do you, like Dad, have a nasty drill sergeant in your head screaming, berating, and belittling you? So, what is the prescription for these foul-mouthed, red-faced, screaming critics full of critical accusations and loathing?

For this deeply insightful and profound answer, I turn to none other than the sugar-loving, Santa-adoring, Code-of-the-Elves-following human, who believed himself to be an elf. Yes, it's Buddy the Elf, who is best known for exclaiming, "The best way to spread Christmas cheer is singing loud for all to hear." In other words, the best way to spread mental and emotional cheer is by encouraging ourselves loudly for *us* to hear.

Buddy faced criticism and negativity at every turn, especially from his biological father, but Buddy knew his identity, he knew his worth, and he rose above the criticism from others. If Buddy can do that with the haters and bah-humbug-ers in his life, we can definitely drown out the drill sergeants, the Grinches, and the Walter Hobbs in our own minds with loud encouragement. We can learn to love ourselves as our neighbors.

We spread mental and emotional cheer by grabbing those pom-poms and channeling our internal cheerleader or Buddy the Elf.

☐ **Recognize and challenge your inner critic**
When the internal drill sergeant screams, "You am such a worthless screwup!" say "I am doing my best and that is enough. I am enough." Replace, "No one will ever love you," with, "I am a valuable person, I have a lot to offer, and I am worthy of love." When he accuses, "You never do anything right and you are messed up beyond saving," exclaim, "I am not defined by my mistakes." (See also Point 5 in chapter 23. These are also helpful in cheering yourself with love, compassion, and grace.)

☐ **Create your own mantra**
One of the most precious and memorable mantras I've ever heard comes from the 2011 film, *The Help.* Aibileen Clark is a black maid hired to care for the affluent Leefolt's home, as well as their sweet, young daughter, Mae Mobley. Witnessing how this little one begins to question her self-worth as a result of her parent's neglect, and verbal and physical abuse, Aiebileen sets out to change her mind in the present with the hope that it will influence how she views herself in the years to come.

During the short time Mae Mobley is in her care, Aibileen consistently and repeatedly affirms her with, "You is kind. You is smart. You is important." It becomes so ingrained in the little girl's mind that upon Aibileen's abrupt termination, she asks Mae Mobley before she leaves, "Do you remember what I told you?" Without missing a beat, the precious little one responds, "You is kind, you is smart, you is important." Aibileen, who was considered "less than" in that time and culture, becomes Mae Mobley's most important (and only) cheerleader and advocate in a home filled with belittling and berating.

You may not have your own personal cheerleader as Mae Mobley did, but you can create or recall a significant affirmation, mantra, or Bible verse that you can repeat to yourself over and over when that cruel drill sergeant is screaming harsh, condemning words in your face.

## ☐ Memorize scriptures and repeat them in times of discouragement and defeat

Even better than a human-made mantra, look to scripture and the words of your heavenly Father who created you and loves you to fight back against the enemy. Here are some that might be helpful.

When you hear, "You am such a worthless screwup," counter with Psalm 139:14, "Thank you for making me so wonderfully complex! Your workmanship is marvelous—how well I know it."

Replace, "No one will ever love you" with Ephesians 2:4-5, "But God is so rich in mercy, and he loved us so much, that even though we were dead because of our sins, he gave us life when he raised Christ from the dead. (It is only by God's grace that you have been saved!)."

When that drill sergeant accuses, "You never do anything right and you're messed up beyond saving," proclaim 1 Peter 2:9, "But you are not like that, for you are a chosen people. You are royal priests, a holy nation, God's very own possession. As a result, you can show others the goodness of God, for he called you out of the darkness into his wonderful light."

So please follow the third commandment and *love yourself as you love your neighbor* today—and always.

Can you hear me, soldier?! I'm cheering for you!

# VII

# I AM PRESENT

*Happy are those who hear the joyful call to worship,*
*for they will walk in the light of your presence, Lord.*
*They rejoice all day long in your wonderful reputation.*
*They exult in your righteousness.*

Psalm 89:15–16

# 25

# "HI, I'M MARTHA. I'M OBSESSIVE COMPULSIVE"

*Be still, and know that I am God.*
Psalm 46:10

"Let's give a big round of applause for Martha and the amazing refreshments for today's meeting of the Shalom Support Group. I've never had matza soup served in a hand-made pottery bowl in the shape of the Sea of Galilee with matza balls shaped like tiny fishing boats."

"Oh, it was nothing. Just something I threw together at the last minute. But I really can't stay for the meeting. So much to do before the Teacher comes to dinner. I'm trimming the myrtle bushes into a topiary of his disciples. I think I'll have them all sitting, rather than reclining. And they'll all be on the same side of the table with the Teacher in the middle. I know! Trend-setting, right?

"Plus I need to stop by the florist for that rose of Sharon and lily of the valley arrangement. Get it? Those are the Teacher's nicknames. I do hope Mary has alphabetized the spices. And Lazarus had better have taken a bath. After four days he smells! I want everything to be just perfect."

And with that Martha was gone.

Yep, Martha in Luke 10:38-42 is the classic Type-A, multitasking control freak we all know—or are. (I are.) Mary is sitting at Jesus' feet, while

Martha is working up a sweat. She complains to him "My sister just sits there while I do all the work."

> But the Lord said to her, "My dear Martha, you are worried and upset over all these details! There is only one thing worth being concerned about. Mary has discovered it, and it will not be taken away from her."

I've described myself as a five-year-old running through an art museum. My goal is to get through the museum as quickly as possible with brief glances at the profound and meaningful works of famous painters. Visit Louvre. Check! Visit the New York Museum of Art. Check! Visit Chicago Art Institute. Check! Instead of sitting and reflecting on the *Mona Lisa, The Starry Night,* or *The Birth of Venus,* I just kept moving! (Well, as a junior-high boy, I did enjoy gazing at the latter painting.\*)

I've always been pedal-to-the-metal, and unfortunately, that has affected my relationships both the earthly and eternal. In *Armchair Mystic: How Contemplative Prayer Can Lead You Closer to God,* Father Mark Thibodeaux describes four stages of intimacy with God:

1. Talking at God
2. Talking to God
3. Listening to God
4. Being with God

As an author and conference speaker, I'm really good at talking *at* and *to* people—and God. That's what I do: I write, you read. I talk, you listen. But one of the great things about the Internet is the ability to have dialog. Readers can respond to my posts with a comment or a LIKE, LOVE, CARE, SAD, or MAD emoji. It's even better at the end of a talk to have time for comments and questions. That's the *listening* part. And if I write with vulnerability and transparency, there can even be a sense of *being with* the reader and listeners.

But to be *with* people and God, I've got to hit life's brakes and be fully present. My very wise five-year-old Faith once told me, "Listen to me with your eyes." (She was already a practicing therapist.) And, I think I've learned that the point of coloring, creating with Play-Doh, and playing Candyland with my wonderful grandchildren is simply being with them— not to create art or play a really boring game. To love them. Encourage them. And to affirm them. "Wow, that is an amazing . . . uh . . . Why don't you tell me what you drew?"

I've tried to shift everything down a few gears. Now instead of inhaling deep-dish pizza, I slowly savor every subtle taste of cheese, tomato sauce, pepperoni, Italian sausage, and parmesan cheese. I thank God for taste buds!

I try to stop and enjoy our row of tiger lilies in front of our house. I marvel at God's bold use of orange and green. So artistic!

And I even try to slow down and enjoy people with their unique and quirky personalities. I thank God for such variety in color, size, shape, and perspectives.

So, this seventy-year-old is deliberately slowing his pace through life. I'm stopping to simply be *with* paintings, people, and God.

* If you didn't have an art appreciation class, *Birth of Venus* by Italian artist Sandro Botticelli, reveals the goddess emerging from a giant clamshell. And yes, she is in her "birthday suit," but her hand and long hair keep the fifth-century painting from earning an R rating.

## PRESCRIPTION

Take a moment—right where you are—to slow down and become more aware, present, and calm in your current space and circumstance. But before you even start this prescription, close your eyes, and take a few deep breaths, focusing on filling your lungs with air as you inhale, and slowly exhale. Next, slowly and intentionally observe or describe what's around you, using your five senses.

☐ **See**

I'm writing this in my favorite coffee shop. I see tables and chairs. The baristas are working quickly to fulfill orders. I see friends meeting together over their drinks. So, what are you observing and noticing with your eyes where you are?

☐ **Smell**

I smell the heavenly aroma of coffee and freshly-baked sweet treats. It's one of my favorite smells in the entire world. What do you smell? Be as perceptive as a crime-scene investigator.

☐ **Touch**

It's a cold, rainy day here in central Indiana—like so many days—so I'm enjoying the warmth of my coffee as I hold the cup between my hands. What are you touching? Take a moment to soak it in.

☐ **Hear**

I hear the grinding of coffee beans, the laughter of friends, and the chit-chat of the baristas as they work together to make drinks and tell stories about their personal lives.

What do you hear? Listen closely. Notice the nuances of each sound.

☐ **Taste**

Of course, I'm drinking one of my favorite go-to caffeinated drinks. I'm tasting the milky, creaminess of my *grande* blonde flat white. I can taste the mellowness of the light roast coffee. What are you tasting? Slow down and enjoy it with every little taste bud in your mouth.

☐ *Be* **present,** *be* **mindful, just** *be*

When you feel overwhelmed with the fast-paced day or you are in super OCD mode to get your to-do list done, take some time to slow down, and even stop where you are and notice every part of your present circumstances using your five senses. Embrace the moment no matter where you are. Stop and smell the roses or the freshly-ground brewed coffee.

# 26

# I AM NOT ANXIOUS— I'M VIGILANT

*Do not be anxious about anything, but in every situation,*
*by prayer and petition, with thanksgiving,*
*present your requests to God.*
Philippians 4:6 NIV

Immediately after the September 11 terrorist attacks, the U.S. Homeland Security created a color-coded threat chart. It ran from "Green" ("No worries, mate!") to "Red" ("We're all going to die!"). Citizens were told not to worry but to "be vigilant." The government finally scrapped the chart because it actually *created* anxiety rather than providing any security.*

So, let's look at the real color codes of life:

## Green: Low Risk

Despite the tragic loss of life on 9/11, those fatalities were just 0.00001 percent or one in one-hundred-thousand people in the United States population. And the odds of dying in any airline accident or attack is one in seven million. So, air travel is solidly "Green: Low."

## Blue: Guarded Risk

Depending on where you were getting your info, the COVID-19 global pandemic's risk lay between "Don't worry. Be happy!" and "Don't buy green bananas!"

To put the pandemic in perspective, you had a one-half of 1 percent chance of dying from COVID compared to 17 percent for heart disease,

135

14 percent for cancer, and 4 percent for lung disease. In other words, a vaccinated person is thirty-four times more likely to die of heart disease than the virus. Twenty-eight times more likely to die of cancer. (Okay, maybe that isn't as comforting as I intended!)

Most of these risks can be reduced to virtually zero by eating right, exercising, getting vaxed and boosted as well as not smoking, vaping, or abusing drugs.

### Yellow: Elevated Risk

The Consumer Product Safery Commission estitmates that around nine-teen-thousand  people lose their lives every year in accidents while in the bathroom, mostly from drowning in the tub. So, relaxing bubble bath: Yellow!

### Orange: High Risk

A 1999 report claimed that ninety-eight thousand hospitalized patients die each year in the United States due to "medical errors." That's equal to over nine-hundred airliner crashes! Orange!

### Red: Severe Risk

The Center for Disease Control reports that each year more than four-hundred-thousand Americans die from cigarette smoking. (That's 133 World Trade Center attacks every year!) Smoking: Red!

Using these statistics, in general, the risk of death in the U.S. of A. is still solidly *green*, but the media has the philosophy of "If it bleeds, it leads!" Granted, "Breaking News: 297 million people in America did not die in an airplane crash this year," would not make great news!

One of the things that keeps me sane—or as close to it as possible—is believing that my life today is solidly *green.* Jesus teaches:

> "So don't worry about these things, saying, 'What will we eat? What will we drink? What will we wear?' These things dominate the thoughts of unbelievers, but your heavenly Father already knows all your needs. Seek

the Kingdom of God above all else, and live righteously, and he will give you everything you need.

"So don't worry about tomorrow, for tomorrow will bring its own worries. Today's trouble is enough for today" (Matthew 6:31–34).

\* According to Chapman University the top ten fears are 1) public speaking, 2) fear of heights, 3) bugs, 4) snakes, 5) drowning, 6) blood/needles, 7) claustrophobia, 8) flying, 9) strangers, and 10) zombies. If you believe zombies are real, you have much bigger problems than fear!

## PRESCRIPTION

Our body's alert system warns of danger, alerting our bodies to fight, flight, and sometimes freeze. Without the amygdala firing on all cylinders in the brains of our cavemen ancestors, alerting them to danger, the population of the world wouldn't have survived past the stone age. Anxiety and the body's physical response are natural responses to a threat and alert us that something is terribly wrong and we are in imminent danger.

Thankfully in the twenty-first century, we don't have to make the life-or-death decisions and face threats that our cavemen ancestors did. I can say with the utmost certainty that most of us didn't step outside our front door this morning worrying that we would be trampled by a herd of charging mastodons.

### ☐ Stop Time Traveling

Unless there is a legitimate threat to our safety through physical violence, sexual assault, or a natural disaster, our anxiety responses—fight, flight, or freeze—are in response to *perceived* threats. These *perceived* threats are most often outside of the realm of the current moment.

Our thoughts, along with Marty McFly, jump into a time-traveling DeLorean and create imagined threats in the future: *I'll never get that job. I'm going to end up living with my parents until I'm fifty.* As terrifying as that sounds, the probability of that happening is very slim and is not an actual threat to our lives.

## ☐ Focus on the facts

Fun fact: "Over 90 percent of the things we worry about don't actually happen." I share this with clients on a weekly basis. Keeping my thoughts in the present has helped me defeat the imaginary saber-toothed tigers in my mind and turned them into cute, cuddly kittens.

## ☐ Practice keeping thoughts in the present

Grounding ourselves in the reality of the moment is a technique we can use in the here and now. Where are you at this current moment? Are you safe? What is the actual threat level? Is it an actual threat to your life or is it a scenario that you have been playing over and over in your mind until it has snowballed and your emotions feel as out of control as an avalanche?

Maybe it's something that, despite desperately wanting to go back and change in your past, you can't. At least not without some plutonium or the 1.21 gigawatts that are needed for time travel.

I find it helpful to box up my thoughts. Does this go in my "Things to think about tomorrow" box? Does this need to be packed away and sealed in the "Things that have already happened and I can't change" box?

## ☐ Follow Jesus's example

Jesus says, "Today's trouble is enough for today." Focus on what you can do today. Be intentional. Do the next best thing today to help you find a career that you love so that you can live independently in the future. In the moment, you can think about ways to forgive yourself and stop beating yourself up over what you said at work yesterday.

"I can let that one go. Chances are, no one will remember it tomorrow, or at least not next year."

"Is there anything I can do today to learn from the mistake I made yesterday?"

Whatever you do, keep your thoughts in today.

☐ **Write these four strategies in your journal. (You *are* journaling, right?) Then write specific ways you can put them into practice.**

# 27

# YOUR MIND ON MINDFULNESS*

*Give your entire attention to what God is doing right now,
and don't get worked up about what may or may
not happen tomorrow. God will help you deal with whatever
hard things come up when the time comes.*
Matthew 6:34 MSG

When Faith and her brother, Paul, were in grade school, they loved Advent calendars. Not only was it a visual way to keep track of how many days until the Christmas-gift-giving extravaganza, but behind each door was a small treat. My wife and I were constantly reminding them to keep tomorrow's door closed.

Today, Faith is a licensed therapist who teaches her clients to keep the door of tomorrow closed as well. In therapy, it's known as mindfulness and has become a hot trend in psychotherapy as an antidote for our distracted, over-stimulated, multitasking, and stress-fueled lives.

*Psychology Today* describes it as "a state of active, open attention on the present. Instead of letting your life pass by you, mindfulness means living in the moment and awakening to experience."

Clinicians are using mindfulness for pain management, addictions, depression, and the general anxiety of life. It's the opposite of multitasking. It's a deliberate living out the moment in the moment.

In fact, mindfulness sounds a lot like *The Message's* paraphrase of Jesus' words at the top of the page.

Kevin Tupper writes at ChristianSimplicity.com:

> Jesus was the most mindful person ever.
>
> He was focused on one thing: the kingdom of God and God's righteousness (Matthew 6:33). That focus shut out petty distractions, diminished worry, and opened him to whatever was happening around him at that moment. Jesus trusted that everything else was in God's hands, and out of his own.

So, it may be a trendy therapy today, but the concept is at least four thousand years old:

> Test me, LORD, and try me,  examine my heart and my mind; for I have always been mindful of your unfailing love and have lived in reliance on your faithfulness (Psalm 26:2–3).

When I'm tempted to freak out, I mentally talk myself off the ledge by meditating on the present moment: "Today, I'm warm and well-fed. I have a roof over my head. I have a reliable vehicle—even if it has over two hundred thousand miles on it. And I am free to write Christian books without the government sending me to a "re-education" camp. Today, everything is great!"

But like commercials, I do need to provide a disclaimer. This doesn't mean I don't pay the mortgage due next week or renew my Internet and cell phone service for another month. I dutifully take care of my earthly responsibilities.

### Wherever I am I am there

If I'm playing a board game with my grandkiddos, I am not thinking, *I really need to be working on that chapter on mindfulness.* When I'm out on a date with my wife, I'm not checking my text messages. It means I'm

not writing a grocery list in the Sermon Notes section of the church bul-
letin. (Okay, sometimes guilty of the grocery list thing.)

God is the only being who can exist in the past, present, and future.
(This may come as quite a shock, but you're not God and neither am I!)
The psalmist writes, "All the days ordained for me were written in your
book before one of them came to be" (Psalms 139:16).

Because *he* holds the future, I can hold today without worry. I can fully
experience and enjoy every person, conversation, situation, and "mega-
meat" pizza. I can enjoy the present because God holds the past and future.

The late Henri Nouwen, in his daily *Meditation,* summed it up well:
"Be sure to taste the moment to the full. The Lord always reveals himself
to you where you are most fully present."

*Some well-meaning Christians associate mindfulness with Zen
Buddhism meditation. However, the Old Testament psalmists promoted
meditation, and Jesus commanded us to be focused on the present rather
than worrying about tomorrow. To reject mindfulness and meditation
because it's a part of eastern belief systems is to reject Chinese food
because it's associated with ancestral worship. Please read the devo-
tion and prescription because there are so many biblical benefits to
mindfulness.

## PRESCRIPTION

Instead of allowing our overwhelming thoughts to snowball, our distressing emotions to spiral out of control, or fighting against the current of
our present reality, we can learn to F-L-O-A-T.

☐ **F-ind your silent place**
Step away from your distressing circumstances and find a quiet place
to remove yourself from the overwhelming situation: your man cave,
she-shed, or maybe even taking a few minutes in the bathroom where
you can find some quiet in the midst of raising toddlers or teenagers.

Jesus modeled this for us when he went to the mountains or gardens to separate himself from the craziness of ministry life and frustrations with shepherding his clueless, ragtag group of disciples.

There are many times though when we can't physically escape to our quiet space. So, let your mind transport you from your current situation to your "silent place," so that you can have some space to calm yourself. Just remember to come back.

### ☐ L-et Go of Judgment

Our thoughts, if left to their own devices, can become very judgmental very quickly, either of ourselves or of others. Judgments always evoke strong emotions, most of the time very negative ones. Just think about the last time you judged someone on social media for their religious or political preferences or even their choice in home décor or parenting decisions. Jesus wants us to let go of critical, emotion-filled judgments so that we can find peace for our troubled minds, overwhelming emotions, and stressed-out bodies in our present moment.

### ☐ O-bserve your thoughts

As I have been writing out these "prescriptions," I hope you are starting to see the power of your thoughts to either destroy you or protect you.

Ignoring thoughts makes them worsen and grow in the darkness of our subconscious.

Fighting thoughts makes them gain more power and have more control of us. Thoughts come and go. They are not permanent.

By observing and becoming more aware of your thoughts, you can start to see them for what they are: just thoughts.

### ☐ A-wareness of your environment

When I sit there in my office staring and dreaming of my tropical happy place, I tap into each of my five senses, focusing on what I was seeing, smelling, hearing, feeling, and tasting there on my private beach. This will help you calm your emotions and make your "happy place" that much richer and more peaceful for your current burnt-out emotions.

□ **T-hankfulness for the experience**

As previously discussed, thankfulness and gratitude can shift our focus and attention. We may be stressed out and overwhelmed with emotions, but we don't have to dwell or ruminate on the struggles of our present moment.

Mindfulness helps us to keep from time traveling and focus on our present moment.

# 28

# IN GOD'S WITNESS PROTECTION PROGRAM

*My old self has been crucified with Christ. It is no longer I who live, but Christ lives in me. So I live in this earthly body by trusting in the Son of God, who loved me and gave himself for me.*
Galatians 2:20

Have you ever dreamed of having a brand-new start: a new name and new location with no "permanent record" of your past?

You can have that if you testify against a powerful crime boss. The United States Marshall's witness protection program* will give you a new name, birth certificate, social security number, new driver's license and passport, move you across the country, and twenty-four-hour protection until you're safe in your "undisclosed location" You have no past except for the new documents provided by the agency. Even a new birth certificate.

Well, God totally trumps the witness protection program. Instead of a new birth certificate, the Bible promises a new *birth* with all our sins expunged from our record. The old you is gone! Check out these liberating promises from God's Word:

> Though we are overwhelmed by our sins, you [Lord] forgive them all (Psalm 65:3).

> "And I will forgive their wickedness, and I will never again remember their sins" (Hebrews 8:12).

But here's another great act that God works in our lives. Not only does he forgive and forget our sins, he also puts us in his witness protection program. We get an entirely new identity!

> Anyone who belongs to Christ has become a new person. The old life is gone; a new life has begun! (2 Corinthians 5:17).

> Let the Spirit renew your thoughts and attitudes. Put on your new nature, created to be like God—truly righteous and holy. (Ephesians 4:23-24).

There are two schools of thought on just how much we are changed. Some believe in the doctrine of imputation, where Christ's atoning blood *covers* our sins. I'm in the impartation camp that believes Christ atoning blood *cleanses* us from sin:

> But if we confess our sins to him, he is faithful and just to forgive us our sins and to *cleanse us from all wickedness* (1 John 1:9, *italics added*).

> Let us go right into the presence of God with sincere hearts fully trusting him. For our guilty consciences have been *sprinkled with Christ's blood to make us clean,* and our bodies have been washed with pure water (Hebrew 10:22, *italics added*).

Yep, when we yield to Christ, we are cleansed, purified, and washed. According to 1 Corinthians 6, the First Church of Corinth was a hot mess of sexual sin, idolatry, adultery, stealing, greed, drunkenness, and abuse. And yet, church-planter Paul writes:

"Some of you were once like that. But you were cleansed; you were made holy; you were made right with God by calling on the name of the Lord Jesus Christ and by the Spirit of our God" (1 Corinthians 6:11).

If you're not already, I would invite you to join God's witness *transformation* program.

\* As of 2020, nineteen-thousand witnesses and family members have been protected since the program began in 1971. Ninety-five percent of those protected are often low-level offenders who testified against higher-level criminals. The Witness Protection Program claims no witnesses have been killed..

## PRESCRIPTION

Katie, a twenty-something, sat on my couch, downcast, in our most recent session last week, discouraged and feeling like there was no point in attending therapy anymore. "Nothing has changed. Is there any point in continuing with therapy?"

I started seeing Katie about three years ago and diagnosed her with bipolar disorder with rapid cycling and psychosis, meaning that her depressive to manic cycles switched very quickly, experiencing the whole emotional gamut, all within five to seven days. (Contrary to popular belief, most true bipolar cycles don't change from moment to moment, but shift every few weeks or sometimes months.)

Her lows have been so low that she is nearly catatonic and unresponsive, having to have her mom dress her and help her move from one room of the house to another. Her highs are extremely high. Think Energizer Bunny after drinking coffee with triple the shots of espresso. Her mania often leads to embarrassing, shameful behavior, such as binge eating, overspending, and hypersexuality.

On this particular day, she was discouraged and overwhelmed with her roller coaster of emotions and wanted to stop the ride. She didn't feel like any of this was helping or that she was making any progress at all. "Nothing has changed."

However, from my vantage point, Katie is not the same girl who came in and sat on my couch three years ago. Katie still struggles with the relentless cycle of bipolar, but she is learning to be mindful and aware of when her emotions and thought processes are slipping into a new gear, either manic or depressive. She can see the mental and emotional warning signs coming and takes action to more effectively handle her highs and lows. And she is committed to growing in her relationship with God and is allowing him to change her from the inside out: a new creation. She is asking life-changing questions that will help you as well. (And remember to write your answers in your journal.)

☐ **How is God changing the way I think?**
How am I looking at or feeling my emotions differently? How are my behaviors and reactions to life circumstances changing? Do I have a clearer vision of his good, pleasing, and perfect will for you? (Romans 12:2).

What are some of the old things I am letting go of and what things am I putting on that reflect a new life growing in me? (2 Corinthians 5:17).

☐ **What new thoughts and attitudes am I putting on?**
How are you relying on the Holy Spirit to do this work in you? How am I becoming more righteous and holy? (Ephesians 4:23–24).

☐ **How is my heart softening?**
Am I letting go of stubbornness, bitterness, resentment, and anger? Am I putting on a more forgiving, tender, and responsive heart? (Ezekiel 11:19).

☐ **Are there specific parts of my life that I have put to death on the cross with Jesus?**
Are there still things I need to lay down at his feet? How have I started to see evidence of Christ living more alive in me? How am I trusting him more? (Galatians 2:20).

☐ **What specific areas of my past need to be brought boldly to him for my conscience to be cleared and guilt and shame erased with his transforming power?**

Have you given yourself over to God's witness protection program? (Hebrew 10:22).

One day we *will* be relocated and utterly transformed for all of eternity. On that day, Katie will be completely released from her roller coaster ride of bipolar. And you will be free of your mental health issue(s)! We can all be part of his Witness *Transformation* Program!

# VIII

# EMPOWERED

*[God] said, "My grace is all you need. My power works best in weakness." So now I am glad to boast about my weaknesses, so that the power of Christ can work through me.*

2 Corinthians 12:9

# 29

# "HI, I'M PETER.
# I'M A TOTAL FAILURE"

*We were crushed and overwhelmed beyond our ability to endure,*
*and we thought we would never live through it.*
2 Corinthians 1:8

"Wow, that was quite a weekend! Unless you've been in *sheol* for the last four days, you know that the miracle-working Yeshua was arrested, crucified, and . . ." The Shalom Support Group leader paused for effect. " . . . raised from the dead. And we have someone in our group who was one of his first disciples who saw him alive the evening of the first day! Peter, tell us all about it. Peter? Peter!"

Peter who had been strangely quiet—the loud and brash disciple had never been quiet—began to sob. He struggled to regain his composure.

"I'm a total failure. I sank when I tried to walk on water. I objected when the Rabbi said he would be executed in Jerusalem. He responded, 'Get behind me, Satan. And then, as I sneaked around outside where he was being tried, I denied I knew him three times. The last time, I Peter the mighty Rock crumbled into grains of sand before a powerless servant.

He buried his face into his hands and began to sob again.

Like Peter, "Christian," the protagonist of John Bunyan's classic *Pilgrim's Progress,*[*] faces his own weaknesses. He confronts challenges and temptations as he makes his way from his home, the City of Destruction, to the Celestial City. All the while, he is carrying a heavy burden.

Christian and one of his traveling companions, Pliable, are chatting away when . . .

> They drew near to a very miry slough that was in the midst of the plain; and they, being heedless, did both fall suddenly into the bog. The name of the slough was Despond. Therefore, they wallowed for a time, being grievously [smeared] with the dirt; and Christian, because of the burden that was on his back, began to sink in the mire.
>
> [Pliable did not sign up for this, so] he gave a desperate struggle or two, and got out of the mire on that side of the slough which was next to his own house: so away he went, and Christian saw him no more. Wherefore Christian was left to tumble in the Slough of Despond alone.

Do you ever feel all alone in your own bog of despondency? Your so-called friends just pull themselves up by their own bootstraps and step out of their emotional swamps and walk away. But we stay stuck. We feel weak. We feel like a failure. We berate ourselves for getting ourselves in the mess and then not being able to fight our way out.

But Help is on the way—literally!

> A man came to him, whose name was Help, and asked him what he did there?
>
> "Sir," said Christian, "I was bid go this way by a man called Evangelist, who directed me also to yonder gate, that I might escape the wrath to come. And as I was going thither, I fell in here."
>
> Then [Help] said, "Give me thy hand." So he gave him his hand, and he drew him out, and set him upon sound ground."

The apostle Paul had fallen in his own slough of despond. But he writes about receiving God's help and now being able to help those in their own slough.

> All praise to God, the Father of our Lord Jesus Christ.
> God is our merciful Father and the source of all comfort.
> He comforts us in all our troubles so that we can comfort
> others. When they are troubled, we will be able to give
> them the same comfort God has given us. For the more
> we suffer for Christ, the more God will shower us with
> his comfort through Christ. Even when we are weighed
> down with troubles, it is for your comfort and salvation!
> For when we ourselves are comforted, we will certainly
> comfort you (1 Corinthians 1:3–6).

Once God—and our therapist—have pulled us out of our slough, we can comfort those weighed down in the mental muck and mire.

Peter goes on to write two letters of encouragement to those facing their own temptations to deny Christ. Paul goes onto to comfort not only the churches he has planted but also two-thousand years of Christ-followers.

Knowing one is not alone is empowering! And we can support those sinking under their own despondency with the comfort we have received. We can be *Help* or direct them to help if we can't personally offer aid.

\* John Bunyan conceived and wrote *The Pilgrim's Progress* while serving twelve years in the Bedford, England, prison. His crime? Being a Baptist "nonconformist preacher," who refused to attend the State's Anglican Church. Bunyan's 1678 book became an instant best-seller and has sold over two-hundred-fifty million copies in over two hundred languages.

## PRESCRIPTION

Have you ever stopped to think about what purpose your present pain might be serving? Or considered how God might use this difficult time to strengthen you or prepare you for something larger than your current pain and suffering? When you find yourself in this "seething caldron of despair," recall times in the past when you can see the purpose that came from your pain.

☐ **Meditate on 2 Corinthians 1:4**

☐ **Honestly answer these questions:**

How can I transform my past or present pain for an eternal purpose?

Who is someone I can comfort despite my own pain?

☐ **Reach out to that someone today. You can be Help!**

# 30

# BREAKING HABITS BEFORE THEY BREAK YOU

*Dear brothers and sisters, if another believer is overcome
by some sin, you who are godly should gently and humbly
help that person back onto the right path.  And be careful not
to fall into the same temptation yourself.*
Galatians 6:1

My Old Testament Survey professor, Wilbur Williams, reminded us, "You can't 'break' the Ten Commandments. They will break you if you disobey them." Good point!

However, I learned the secret to breaking habits in high school journalism class. Mrs. Leiter demanded that every hard-news story contain five *W*'s and an *H*.

## Who?

Jeremy used to limp into my office once a week. "I'm so discouraged. I gave in and smoked weed again. I went over to Tim's to share Jesus with my old friends, and before I knew it, I had a joint in my hand."

If every time you're with a particular person you start smoking weed, cutting down people, drinking, going too far sexually, or [fill in the habit], you need to limit your time with him or her.

## Where?

Have you noticed that certain locations create different moods—school creates boredom, sitting in the kitchen makes you hungry, and trying to do work in bed makes you sleepy?

The same principle works for habits.

Ray used to sneak down to the basement for a bottle of wine hidden behind the furnace.

"It was really weird, Pastor Jim. I thought I had beaten my urge to drink. But today, when I was helping my dad change furnace filters, that temptation came back really bad!"

So, if at all possible, stay clear of those locations that tempt you or where you used to engage in that habit. If it's a place you absolutely can't avoid such as the bathroom, at least be on your guard. Temptation is going to be particularly strong there! But each time you *don't* give in there, you will start to break that association with the habit and that location.

## When?

Have you noticed that temptations seem greater at certain times? Maybe it's the time of day or when you're tired, worried, depressed, or not feeling well. (I get tempted to eat my body weight in dark chocolate when I'm depressed or bored.)

Obviously, you can't change monthly cycles, the time of day, weather, or your health. But you *can* be aware of when temptation seems to be strongest—and be prepared for it.

## How?

God wants to help us meet that need. Habits only give us temporary relaxation, security, or release from frustration. But a relationship with God can provide a permanent solution.

He'll probably help us through people in our church, youth group, or small group Bible study. First Corinthians 10:13 encourages us that we are not alone in our temptations. Look to Christian friends for support and prayer.

## Why?

Real success begins with the question of why. Try to discover what need you're trying to satisfy by indulging in the habit. Be honest.

Sheila confessed that she was hooked on sex. She didn't care who the guy was or if she really liked him. Most of her time had been spent hanging out in bars waiting for someone to pick her up for a "one-nighter."

As we talked, she poured out her unhappy childhood. "I never remember my parents ever hugging me or telling me that they loved me. I craved for someone—anyone—to hold me and tell me they loved me. It didn't matter if they meant it or not. I just wanted to hear it."

Sheila began to feel accepted by the church's small group and sensed unconditional love from the leaders and members. The void was now being filled in a positive, safe way.

So, please remember: You *can* break habits before they break you!

\* Dr. Meg Arroll, a chartered psychologist with the British Psychological Society, studied two thousand Brits to discover their top ten bad habits: 1) comfort eating, 2) swearing, 3) biting nails, 4) not doing exercise, 5) procrastinating, 6) stressing about things, 7) nose-picking, 8) eating fast food, 9) snoozing alarm, and 10) spending too long scrolling through social media. The study also revealed that the average person has three bad habits of the fifty identified.

## PRESCRIPTION

I don't know much about plants, but I do seem to have an uncanny ability to grow weeds. Maybe you feel the same way about life. The weeds have been growing out of control, choking out the beauty of your life and all that you want to become. In the garden of our souls, we have to rid our lives of weeds that are a hindrance in order to create a beautiful life worth living.

☐ **Clear the weeds**

On the surface of our lives are the people, places, and things that cause us problems. Take a moment to list the people, places, and things that lead you to do the things that choke out your life. When are the times that you are most vulnerable to negative emotions or decisions? For each "weed" make a specific plan to rid yourself or make yourself less vulnerable in those specific moments.

☐ **Remove the weeds by the root**

In the process of removing the weeds, we have to get below the surface to the life source of the weed and destroy the roots. Our negative, faulty beliefs, thoughts, and emotions have to be "Round-Up" and identified before we can rid ourselves of them. *What are the losses and hurts in my past that continue to control my thoughts, emotions, and actions today?* Write your thoughts in your journal and talk these through with someone you trust.

☐ **Replace barren, depleted soil with fertile, nutrient-rich soil**

Removing weeds by the roots isn't enough to experience life change. We have to replace the old, deteriorated soil with new life-giving beliefs, thoughts, and ways to manage our emotions to keep the foundation of our lives healthy and nutrient-rich. This final step is ongoing as we seek to change our emotional patterns, reactions, and long-term negative habits over the long haul. This step can be a difficult one and is most effective when done with an accountability partner, a support group, or a licensed therapist.

☐ **Plant life-giving people, places, and things**

Getting rid of ugly weeds isn't enough. We must plant beautiful flowers in place of the weeds. Otherwise, we will be left with a void in our lives that we will want to refill with our bad habits. What life-giving people, places, and things do I need to incorporate into my life that will encourage me in my new positive habits and to grow an award-winning flower bed? Identify how each one will specifically play a role in developing a new way of responding or reacting. Make a specific plan for how you will go about planting these beautiful "flowers" into your life.

Be empowered and know that even if all you've been able to grow are weeds up to this point in your life, you *can* become a master gardener and the proud owner of a *Better Homes and Gardens*-worthy flower bed. You can create a beautiful life worth living!

# 31

# DEPRESSION IS
# MY SUPERPOWER

*He gives power to the weak and strength to the powerless.*
Isaiah 40:29

Superheroes have become, well, "super" in surprising ways. Spiderman was bitten by a radioactive spider. The Hulk also gained his superpowers from radiation exposure. The Green Lantern discovered a magical ring. Batman and Iron Man get their powers from cutting-edge technology. Wolverine has medical implants while Captain America was injected with "Super-Soldier" serum. And Catwoman suffered a head injury in a plane crash.

My superpowers come from clinical depression. Yep, university studies have shown that just like fictional superheroes, people with clinical depression have real skills and abilities superior to so-called "normal" people.[*] (I'll drop a load of scientific studies on you just to prove I'm making this stuff up!)

## Creativity

As far back as 500 BC, normal people have suspected a link between creative people and mental health issues. Greek philosopher Aristotle wrote that authors and artists all have tendencies toward "melancholia" or depression.

According to Sweden's Karolinska Institute, creativity is "akin to insanity." Brain scans reveal, and I quote, "striking similarities in the thought pathways of highly creative people and those with schizophrenia. Both groups lack important receptors used to filter and direct thought."

The Swedish study also notes this allows creative people to think outside the box. The institute's Fredrik Ullen discovered that both highly creative people and those with schizophrenia had "a lower degree of signal filtering, and thus a higher flow of information" in the brain. So, there is a real reason I keep saying offensive stuff. I have a defective filter!

Mark Millard, a member of the British Psychological Society, believes, and I quote, "this barrage of uncensored information . . . ignites the creative spark. This would explain how highly creative people manage to see unusual connections in problem-solving situations that other people miss."

### Sense of humor?

Do depressed people make better comics? Just look at all the modern comedians who have admitted to dealing with depression: Woody Allen, Wayne Brady, Drew Carey, Jim Carrey, Rodney Dangerfield, Larry David, David Letterman, and Robin Williams. Chris Rock calls comedy "the blues for people who can't sing."

However, famous psychiatrist Sigmund Freud in his 1905 book, *Jokes and Their Relation to the Unconscious,* argued "humor is the highest of the psyche's defense mechanisms, capable of turning anxiety into pleasure." Psychologist and former stand-up comic, Dr. Nancy Irwin, agrees: "Humor is actually one of the highest forms of defense mechanisms to cope with pain."

So, I'm putting a question mark behind "Sense of Humor." While many of the funniest people are depressed, it seems to be a *defense mechanism against the depression* that creates the laughs, *not the depression itself.* And the suicides of comedians such as Robin Williams warn us that defense mechanisms, rather than treatment, can be deadly.

Make people laugh—and take your Prozac!

### Empathy

*Frontiers in Psychology* published a study by Yuan Cao and three of his colleagues at the School of Psychology at the University of Queensland,

Australia. Cao writes, "Previous studies have shown changes in empathy in patients with depression, including an elevated level of trait personal distress."

While the study was specifically looking at unhealthy "empathetic distress," it did validate earlier studies showing an increase in empathetic response in those with depression.

Charles Spurgeon writes about his empathy toward those suffering from depression:

> I often feel very grateful to God that I have undergone fearful depression of spirits. I know the borders of despair, and the horrible brink of that gulf of darkness into which my feet have almost gone; but hundreds of times I have been able to give a helpful grip to brethren and sisters who have come into that same condition, which grip I could never have given if I had not known their deep despondency. So, I believe that the darkest and most dreadful experience of a child of God will help him to be a fisher of men if he will but follow Christ.

So, I am grateful for clinical depression, which has made me more creative, possibly more humorous, and definitely more empathetic.

But a note of caution: While it seems people with depression often show these characteristics, too much of a good thing can be detrimental. That's why mental health issues must be viewed on a spectrum from healthy to unhealthy. Too much creativity and a mad scientist may emerge. King Agrippa tells the apostle Paul that too much deep thinking and study has made him "mad." And too much empathy can be emotionally crippling while sociopathic serial killers have no empathy. Any extreme can be detrimental, so strive for balance.

And, remember the sage advice of Spiderman's uncle: "With great power comes great responsibility."

\* One of my favorite bits of wisdom is Patsy Clairmont's book title: *Normal Is Just a Setting on Your Dryer.* Patsy admits to being agoraphobic. (Mayo Clinic describes it as "a type of anxiety disorder in which you fear and avoid places or situations that might cause you to panic and make you feel trapped, helpless, or embarrassed.") And yet she has traveled around the world as a popular speaker and author encouraging people that *God Uses Cracked Pots.*

## PRESCRIPTION

We have one more secret power at our disposal: our *suffering.* Say what? When we are in the thick of our difficult circumstances and emotions, we are definitely *not* thinking about how surviving our current pain and heartache will make us a stronger, better person in the future.

I know for a fact that when I was in my seasons of deep grief, pain, and anxiety, I was for sure *not* thinking to myself, *This is such a wonderful experience. Just think of all the comfort I'll be able to give others when this is all over* [Insert eye roll.]

But looking back, God used those dark places to create in me a deeper love and compassion for the betrayed, the single mom, the broken, the addicted, and yes, even the cheating spouse. What I thought would kill me, gave me a platform to spread encouragement and hope to a hurting world. Think of it this way:

**Strengths + Spiritual gifts + Suffering = Superpowers**

☐ **In what ways is God using your painful past and suffering to make you more like Christ? Through your suffering, are you becoming more loving, generous, forgiving, patient, humble, or any of the other character traits of Jesus?**

☐ How has suffering made you more grateful for the suffering Jesus experienced on the cross for you so that you could have eternal life and use your superpowers for him?

☐ Be the super hero you were created to be!

# 32

# I'VE FALLEN, AND I CAN GET UP

*[God] gives power to the weak and strength to the powerless. . . .*
*Those who trust in the Lord will find new strength.*
*They will soar high on wings like eagles. They will run and*
*not grow weary. They will walk and not faint.*
Isaiah 40:29, 31

D
o you remember the LifeCall commercial with Mrs. Fletcher's classic line, "I've fallen and I can't get up!"* Its terrible acting has been parodied and mocked in print, TV, and online! But the good news is that if we've fallen, we *can* get up.

## Getting Up Psychologically

Another great slogan for which I'm grateful is an old Dow Chemical commercial from the past century: "Better Living Through Chemistry." Yep, if it weren't for two prescription drugs for my clinical depression, I would be in bed, under the covers, and eating my body weight in dark chocolate rather than writing this book.

Mental health treatment has advanced from exorcisms, frontal lobotomies, and electro-convulsive shock treatments. So, I hope you've talked to your primary care physician, a licensed therapist, or another mental health professional about your particular issue to see if a psychotropic drug may help.

Don't let the label "psychotropic" freak you out. It has nothing to do with "psycho" as in serial killer. It simply means "A drug or other substance that affects how the brain works and causes changes in mood, awareness, thoughts, feelings, or behavior."

The good kinds are medications for depression, anxiety, bipolar, etc. The bad kinds are alcohol, street drugs, or any prescription that is abused. Since many psychiatric conditions are caused by some kind of chemical imbalance in the brain, modern medicine has developed medications to treat many of those imbalances.

A friend who was hearing voices convinced herself she was demon-possessed. However, a prescription of Haldol exorcized those "demons."

Xanax is the most popular psychotropic drug with over forty-eight million users, and is prescribed for symptoms of anxiety, panic disorder, and anxiety associated with depression by producing a calming effect on the patient. (That's not surprising in a culture that is certifiably stressed out!) It does have very serious side effects, so discuss it honestly with your medical professional.

Zoloft, with forty-one million users, comes in a strong second as the most popular medication for clinical depression. It's believed to be caused by a decrease of the chemical serotonin which transmits signals between neurons in the brain. Selective serotonin uptake inhibitors can increase the levels needed for a healthy brain. Other antidepressants include Celexa, Cymbalta, Lexapro, Paxil, Prozac, and Wellbutrin. Many people may need to try several types before finding the most effective medication for them. I did.

My publisher's lawyer insists I warn you that these are powerful drugs and should not be shared with others, bought on the Internet, and/or never used without the supervision of a mental health professional.

### Getting Up Physically, Socially, Mentally, Spiritually

My publisher's lawyer also wants me to write in capital letters and in bold font:

## Drugs are not a cure-all!

For instance, my antidepressants give me that extra bit of strength and motivation to eat right, exercise, and think on those things that are "true, and honorable, and right, and pure, and lovely, and admirable" (Philippians 4:8). Without the drugs, I'd still be under the covers!

Humans are holistic beings with physical, social, mental, and spiritual elements interacting with each other. So, talking with a trained therapist can help you in all areas of your life. Diet and exercise can also have an effect on your mental health (Yeah, yeach, yeah. It always comes back to diet and exercise doesn't it?)

Treatment options can include:

Online groups and forums can be filled with all kinds of misinformation from people who should not be allowed access to the Internet. (Make sure the forum is moderated by a mental health professional.)

Self-diagnosis and especially self-medicating can be dangerous and deadly. (Yeah, our lawyer also wanted me to stress that "Dr. Google" can be a quack.)

There are trained peer counselors, licensed therapists, and inpatient programs to help you avoid the final form of treatment: the psychiatric prison.

There is hope. You *can* get up!


\* While preparing to film the original LifeCall commercial in 1989, Edith Fore , who portrayed the fallen woman, suggested the now-famous line. Unfortunately, LifeCall went out of business in 1993 and couldn't get up.


## PRESCRIPTION

How do we know when our everyday feelings have become more pervasive and problematic? Our everyday feelings are ever-changing from moment to moment, but if you have noticed that your difficult feelings have become longer-lasting and are persistent over days, weeks, or months, it might be time to consider scheduling with a therapist and making an appointment with your doctor.

☐ **Take a moment to thoughtfully read and check any symptoms that you are currently experiencing**

☐ Feelings of sadness, tearfulness, emptiness, or hopelessness

☐ Angry outbursts, irritability, or frustration, even over small matters

☐ Loss of interest or pleasure in most or all normal activities, such as sex, hobbies, or sports

☐ Sleep disturbances, such as difficulty falling or staying asleep, restlessness, unsatisfying sleep, or sleeping too much.

☐ Tiredness and lack of energy, so even small tasks take extra effort; being easily fatigued.

☐ Reduced appetite and weight loss or increased cravings for food and weight gain

☐ Anxiety, agitation or restlessness, feeling wound up, or on edge.

☐ Difficulty controlling feelings or thoughts of worry.

☐ Slowed thinking, speaking, or body movements

☐ Feelings of worthlessness or guilt, fixating on past failures or self-blame

☐ Trouble thinking, concentrating, making decisions, remembering things, or mind going blank.

☐ Frequent or recurrent thoughts of death, suicidal thoughts, suicide attempts, or suicide

☐ Unexplained physical problems, such as back pain, headaches, or muscle tension.

If you marked any of these symptoms and are noticing that they have lasted more than a month and are affecting various areas of your life . . .

☐ **Make the call today. It's time to get back up!**

## IX

# I AM VICTORIOUS

*For God has not given us a spirit of fear and timidity,*
*but of power, love, and self-discipline.*

2 Timothy 1:7

# 33

# "HI, I'M LEE. I HAVE SELF-CONTROL ISSUES"

*Overwhelming victory is ours through Christ.*
Romans 8:37

The new person at the Shalom Support Group looked as if he had just come from a bar brawl. Bandages bound his wrists and deep purple bruises covered his face.

"Hi, I'm Jacob, and I facilitate this group. We're so glad to have you here. Would you like to introduce yourself?"

"Hi, I'm Lee. I have self-control issues."

"Wait! Are you Lee from Decapolis? Do you go by the nickname Legion? I didn't recognize you with your clothes on."

Immediately, those in the group began nervously eyeing the exit. Everyone had read the stories. "This man lived in the burial caves and could no longer be restrained, even with a chain. Whenever he was put into chains and shackles—as he often was—he snapped the chains from his wrists and smashed the shackles. No one was strong enough to subdue him. Day and night he wandered among the burial caves and in the hills, howling and cutting himself with sharp stones" (Mark 5:3–5).

"Yeah, but not to worry. Just recently, I met the promised Messiah, and he freed me from all my demons." Lee paused a second, then smirked. "And in the process, he also created deviled ham!"

The group groaned.

"Well, I guess he didn't cast out my bad jokes, but let me tell you what he did do for me . . ."

While I was undergoing radiation treatments for cancer, I was scheduled to speak at a large conference. My strength was totally, completely depleted, not a drop of gas in the tank—not even fumes. I had no idea how I was going to have the energy to present the closing keynote address. As I sat in the front row listening to my introduction, I inwardly screamed, *I cannot do this!* But immediately, God seemed to say, "That's exactly what I needed to hear."

God promises us victory at the point where we seem to be completely depleted and defeated. (The Bible is filled with hundreds of examples!) St. Paul wanted to convey this powerful truth, but he was at a loss for words. So, he just made up a word.

> We are more than conquerors through him who loved
> us (Romans 8:37).

The words translated "more than conquerors" is actually a mashup of two Greek words: *hyper* and *nike.*

If you or your child has ADHD (Attention-deficit/hyperactivity disorder), there's no need for a description. *Hyper* means "over the top," "above and beyond." And we all recognize the word *nike* from the famous athletic wear and the Greek goddess of victory, although the original pronunciation is "nik-ay.

As I weakly made my way to the stage, I was immediately filled with over-the-top energy for the forty-minute talk. In fact, it was one of my most energized and Spirit-empowered talks ever! But as soon as I sat back down, the exhaustion instantly returned. God had provided *hyper nike* just when I needed it!

No matter what mental health challenge you are facing, God wants to do that for you as well. That's why Paul writes: "That's why I take pleasure in my weaknesses,* and in the insults, hardships, persecutions, and troubles that I suffer for Christ. For when I am weak, then I am strong" (2 Corinthians 12:10).

"Wait a minute, Mr. Smarty Pants author! You want me to take pleasure in my mental health condition that keeps me from doing the things I would like to do? You want me to take pleasure in hurtful insults that have taunted me all of my life? You want me to take pleasure in the bullying I have faced since the first day of school? With all due respect, your ink well isn't filled to the top."

Well, just look at who is writing this book! In college "Freshman Composition" and "Creative Writing" I got C's. Now I have twenty traditionally-published books and nearly three thousand articles, scripts, poems, and short stories in print which have won numerous national awards. And guess who taught writing at a prestigious university for fifteen years? Yep, the guy with the C's in college writing! Yeah, ca-razy!

And who is smiling—mischievously—when I seem to be having a real impact on the lives of those who read my books and hear me speak? God! He gets the glory for making each of us super victors despite our challenges.

So, yeah, I take pleasure in my weaknesses.

\* Theologians love to speculate what was Paul's "thorn in the flesh" (2 Corinthians 12:7). Theories include chronic eye problems, epilepsy, malaria, migraines, opposition from Jewish religious leaders, persecution, a speech disability, and—shall we say—a strong libido.

### PRESCRIPTION

God uses our weakness for his glory through the work of the holy spirit. I want you to live a life infused with his "super-nike" giving spirit as you tap into this mysterious process of his power working in your weakness. Say these statements out loud to him and be strengthened with his encouragement through the Word and the **S-P-I-R-I-T**.

☐ **S-urrender**
God, I can't do this on my own. I don't have the power to do this.

"The Lord hears his people when they call to him for help. He rescues them from all their troubles. The Lord is close to the broken-hearted; he rescues those whose spirits are crushed" (Psalm 34:17–18).

## ☐ P-ray for strength
Give me your power through the Holy Spirit.

"In the same way, the Spirit also helps our weakness; for we do not know how to pray as we should, but the Spirit Himself intercedes for us with groanings too deep for words" (Romans 8:26 NIV).

## ☐ I-nvite him into your situation
Come into this situation. I desperately need you.

"Don't be afraid, for I am with you. Don't be discouraged, for I am your God. I will strengthen you and help you. I will hold you up with my victorious right hand" (Isaiah 41:10).

## ☐ R-est in his strength
Help me experience your power and strength right now.

"But those who trust in the Lord will find new strength. They will soar high on wings like eagles. They will run and not grow weary. They will walk and not faint" (Isaiah 40:31).

## ☐ I- can do all things!
I can do all things with your strength.

"This is my command—be strong and courageous! Do not be afraid or discouraged. For the Lord, your God is with you wherever you go" (Joshua 1:9).

## ☐ T-hank him for his strength
Thank you for helping me through that situation. I couldn't have done it without you.

"The Lord is my strength and my song; he has given me victory.

This is my God, and I will praise him—my father's God, and I will exalt him!" (Exodus 15:2).

Go forward in your day knowing that you are "more than a conqueror" and an "over-the-top victor" through the power and strength of the S-P-I-R-I-T.

# 34

# EMOTIONS REAL, BUT NOT REALITY

*God is greater than our feelings.*
1 John 3:20

During the American Civil War, the Confederate Navy filled Mobile Bay on the Gulf of Mexico with mines, which at the time were called "torpedoes." As flag officer David Glasgow Farragut led the Union's fleet of eighteen ships into the bay, he issued one of history's most memorable orders:

"D--- the torpedoes! Full speed ahead!"

The tactic succeeded. Only one ship was lost, and the last Confederate stronghold on the Gulf of Mexico fell to Union control. (And Farragut was made admiral of the U.S. Navy and honored with two postage stamps.) It's also a good strategy for our emotions:

## Don't deny emotions

I'm certainly not denying that my life is a mine-filled sea of emotions. I regularly struggle with *clinical depression* so there are days I just want to run below deck, hide in the hull, eat my body weight of dark chocolate, and write awful poetry. But I'm not alone. I have plenty of company with the psalmists of the Bible. One-third of all psalms are known as "laments," which is just a theological word for *whining*.

> My God, my God, why have you abandoned me?
> Why are you so far away when I groan for help?

Every day I call to you, my God, but you do not answer.
Every night you hear my voice, but I find no relief
(Psalm 22:1–2).

O God, why have you rejected us so long?
Why is your anger so intense against the sheep of your
own pasture? (Psalm 74:1).

When I was in deep trouble,
I searched for the Lord.
All night long I prayed, with hands lifted toward heaven,
but my soul was not comforted (Psalm 77:2).

## Don't deify emotions

The psalmists certainly didn't deny their emotions, but neither did that make their emotions their god. Inevitably, the psalms above were followed by a psalm of praise:

The Lord is my shepherd;
I have all that I need.
He lets me rest in green meadows;
he leads me beside peaceful streams (Psalm 23:1–2).

We thank you, O God!
We give thanks because you are near.
People everywhere tell of your wonderful deeds
(Psalm 75:1).

Saint Paul sums up these "bi-polar" extremes of emotions:

We are pressed on every side by troubles, but we are
not crushed. We are perplexed, but not driven to despair.

We are hunted down, but never abandoned by God. We get knocked down, but we are not destroyed (2 Corinthians 4:8–9).

## Do defy emotions

Emotions are fickle feelings that may be caused by chemical imbalances in the brain, a subconscious reaction to an event in the past or present, or perhaps something we ate the night before. Emotions are real, but they are not reality. (You may want to write that down and post it on the bathroom mirror!)

So, I find myself paraphrasing Admiral Farragut's order: "D--- the emotions! Full speed ahead!"

And most days, I'm successful in navigating the emotional mines floating in my life with prayer, persistence, and Prozac. I can't deny them, but I also refuse to deify them. They are not my God, but biochemicals, subconscious reactions or, perhaps, the pizza I ate before bed.

Full speed ahead!

## PRESCRIPTION

Emotions have gotten a bad rap since the beginning of time. Most of my clients come to therapy because they have been avoiding feelings, negatively expressing feelings, sometimes to the point of being completely controlled by their emotions, or they just don't have the emotional vocabulary to talk about them in a helpful, healing way. Below is a way that you can start having more mastery in this area of your life.

### ☐ Acknowledge and accept your feelings

What am I feeling? What happened that triggered this emotion? What thoughts and beliefs triggered this emotion? How was I feeling this emotion in my body? What did I feel like doing or do?

☐ **Consider if your emotions are a real assessment or something else**
Was my response effective or in the reality of the experience? Were my thoughts justifiable by facts? Were my feelings based on faulty perceptions or misinterpretations or were they justified?

☐ **If they are not, challenge each of your *feel* statements with a *know* statement followed by the evidence for that statement**
Consider the evidence. For example, we may *feel* very deeply that, "Everybody hates me, nobody likes me." But when we balance this statement with the facts, we find that in reality, there are many people who love and care about us. Instead, challenge it with, "I may *feel* like no one loves me, but I *know* that my mom, sister, and husband love me. They have always been there for me when I really needed encouragement."

☐ **If they are real, face them**
Defying our emotions allows us to experience and embrace our feelings, but also to render them powerless to control us. Problem-solving helps us know how to best manage what we are feeling. What is the most effective way I can face this? I suggest keeping a mood journal, deep breathing, talking to someone, giving yourself some space to step back and reflect, or . . .

☐ **Meditate on God's Word and his truths about our emotions**
Dad offered some emotion-focused scriptures here. God's Word is filled with emotion-challenging, emotion-facing truths that we can use to defy overwhelmed emotions.

☐ **Write "Emotions are real, but not reality" on a Post-It** (Thanks, Dad!)

# 35

# HI, I'M JIM. I HAVE AN ADDICTIVE PERSONALITY

*You say, "I am allowed to do anything"—but not everything is good for you. And even though "I am allowed to do anything," I must not become a slave to anything.*
1 Corinthians 6:12

As I loaded up our car for the recycle center, I discovered that ten large trash bags of Diet Coke cans wouldn't fit in the trunk, backseat, and passenger front seat. At that moment, I thought, *I may have a problem.* "Duh. Da ya think?"

Yep, I was up to eight to ten cans per day.

And I wasn't any better with dark chocolate.* And I wasn't messing around with gateway milk or white chocolate. No, I was going for uncut Dove and Ghirardelli 75 percent dark with at least a dozen or more hits a day! (Fortunately, I had not started mainlining Hershey syrup—yet.)

Based on the DSM, signs of addiction to anything from porn to pot are:

☐ Cravings to use the substance.

☐ Wanting to cut down or stop but not managing to.

☐ Taking the substance in larger amounts or for longer than you meant to.

☐ Neglecting other parts of your life because of substance abuse.

☐ Continuing to use, even when it causes problems in relationships.

☐ Using substances even when it puts you in danger.

The first three? Check. Check. Check. But my justification was that I wasn't hooked on heroin or stealing from my family to support my habit. (Okay, Faith reminded me that I would go through her and her brother's trick-or-treat candy and pilfer all the miniature dark chocolate bars. Busted!)

However, after ten cans of Diet Coke and handfuls of Dove chocolate per day, I had the heart rate and blood pressure of a hummingbird. Number six? Check.

## Life, liberty, love

God's desire for his beloved children boils down to three things: to be engaged in only those things that promote life, liberty, and love. It's not about taking "bad" things out of our life but replacing them with "good" things. In fact, the United States' Declaration of Independence argues that life and liberty are inalienable rights for all people, and the Beatles sing that all you need is love. Good theology!

[The enemy's] "purpose is to steal and kill and destroy. My purpose is to give them a rich and satisfying *life*" (Jesus, John 10:10, *italics added*).

Stand firm therefore in the *liberty* by which Christ has made us free, and don't be entangled again with a yoke of bondage (Galatians 5:1 *World English Bible*, *italics added*).

> [All the commandments] are summed up in this one
> commandment: "Love your neighbor as yourself." Love
> does no wrong to others, so *love* fulfills the requirements
> of God's law (Romans 13:9–10, *italics* added).

Those three filters—life, liberty, and love—have changed how I live my life physically, mentally, and spiritually. So rather than concentrating on *not* doing certain things, I focused on *doing* life, liberty, and love.

So, I've switched to ice water with lemon and limit myself to just eight pieces of Dove throughout the day. My blood pressure is 116 over 68 and my heart rate is down to sixty now. And I've lost sixteen pounds—or two gallons of blubber—in two and a half months. Just fourteen pounds to go. And I do feel so much better.

While our enemy promises freedom to do whatever we want, his real purpose is to kill our bodies, steal our freedom, and to destroy relationships. "Instead of enjoying the fleeting pleasures of sin" (Hebrews 11:25), Jesus invites us to "rich and satisfying" years with life, liberty, and love.

\* In my defense, let the record show that according to scientific, peer-reviewed studies by major universities and hospitals—I'm not making this up—dark chocolate is actually good for you! It decreases blood pressure, increases blood flow, reduces heart disease risk, relieves stress, improves cognitive function, and contains antioxidants that can reduce cholesterol, age-related macular degeneration, and even cancer! However, medical researchers stress moderate intake. Sigh. Plus, there are no medical benefits from white chocolate (an oxymoron) and milk chocolate, which are high in sugar.

## PRESCRIPTION

I first met Ben when he was freshly bonded out of jail where he had served thirty days but was facing a twenty-plus-year sentence because of his recent drug charge. Just a few weeks prior to sitting in my office, he had an encounter with Jesus while sitting alone in his isolation cell at the county lockup, and he was ready to get his life back. It was in my office that he shared his story of brokenness:

> Just last month, I was arrested for dealing and possession of heroin. I have been arrested for two driving-under-the-influence charges with marijuana, cocaine, crystal meth, and heroin. I have had a drug problem for twenty-five years. During my last arrest, I lay in intake for days with no food or water. I wanted to lay there and die.

Ben's story was definitely *not* one of life, liberty, and love. Ben's using behavior fit every one of the criteria for an addictive disorder: Cravings to do the behavior? Check! Wanting to cut down or stop but not managing to? Check! Taking things further than you intended to? Check! Neglecting other parts of your life? Check! Continuing to do the behavior even when it's causing problems? Check! Doing the behavior even when it puts you in danger? Check!

The nature of addiction is that as hard as people try, as much as they will themselves to do things differently this time, they always do what they don't want to do, and they don't do what they want to do.

But Ben desperately wanted to live in peace, and yet there was a war inside of him wreaking havoc on his mind, body, and soul. While still in jail, Ben had an encounter with God. He noticed a calming change come over his body, and his attitude and mindset changed. He found inner strength that he had never felt before. Ben knew when he got out of jail, he was going to do whatever God wanted him to do. It was there in jail that he started his journey of recovery.

### Admit there's a problem.

Ben's narrative began to change the minute he admitted that this was not the life he wanted to live. He hit his rock bottom there in that jail cell. His drug of choice was heroin, but if we are honest, we all have drugs of choice: money, shopping, working, hobbies, romantic relationships, gambling, porn, sex, food, or our phone.

Take a moment to think about something in your life that seems to be robbing you of your life, liberty, or love. Take a moment to look at these symptoms of addiction, ask God to show you any addictive behaviors, and mark any that apply.

☐ Cravings to do the behavior?

☐ Wanting to cut down or stop but not managing to?

☐ Taking things further than you intended to?

☐ Neglecting other parts of your life?

☐ Continuing to do the behavior even when it's causing problems?

☐ Doing the behavior even when it puts you in danger?

## Believe

If you marked any of these, there are some addictive behaviors in your life that need to be addressed.

Thankfully for Ben and the millions of people caught in some kind of addictive behavior and patterns, there is hope, and there can be healing. Ben found this hope in of all places, a jail cell.

I had a visitor come who asked me about my relationship with God and where I would spend eternity. I knew the answer. I sat in my cell and cried out for God to bring mercy to my soul. I told God, "Use me, Lord. I'm tired of messing up. I can't do it alone. I have tried so many times and I surrender to you God. Please help me."

If you are tired of doing the same thing over and over expecting different results, and you are longing for a life full of freedom and love, write a letter to Jesus about where you are and where you want to be. Believe and surrender your life and your addiction to him.

## Commit

Simply admitting and believing isn't enough. We have to commit to the change process and take action. In jail, Ben committed his life to Jesus and a new life of recovery began. He shared his reflections as he graduated from the program and said goodbye to the group:

> My recovery starts with Jesus. I have given my life to him and started a recovery plan. I have attended a meeting every day since being out of jail. I have several friends in recovery who made things easy for me. They welcomed me with love and hugs. I took all the suggestions that were given to me, and these became tools in my recovery. I stopped doing things for myself. It is said that you only keep what you have by giving it away. Life is no longer about me. It is about what God wants me to do. I get to speak to others and share my experience, strength, and hope. I believe in myself today. There is no going backward for me. What I have learned is it's not about being clean. It's about being a better person and giving back. God put me on a journey. I see myself as a recovery rock star, I love myself, and I love Jesus. Grateful to be clean. Grateful for the wisdom I have. Grateful to have a choice. I am extremely blessed. Jesus carried the cross on his shoulders so I could start over.

☐ **Commit your addictive behaviors to God**

He is the one who brings abundant life, joyous freedom, and everlasting love. Tell him the specific steps you are committing to today. Make a list so that you can see this as a reminder in black and white of the commitment you are making. And then tell someone else your plan for accountability.

## ☐ Keep at it one day at a time

Recovery takes a one-day-at-a-time approach. It is about living in the here and now and choosing the next best thing moment by moment until we can look back and see just how far we've come. I have had the privilege of running into Ben every now and then out in the community. Seeing the transformation that has taken place in him day after day, year after year, is astonishing. He is truly experiencing a new life, liberty, and love.

> I've been clean since November 2015. Over the years, I've shared my testimony in numerous churches, as well as in recovery groups, about the transformational power of God. I have even been blessed to share my story on CBN's *The 700 Club.*
>
> I'm currently a supervisor of a sober living home in my community. I try to minister everywhere I go, sharing the good news of the gospel. I have passed from death to life and couldn't live the life I do today without Christ! Ever since that day I made my covenant with God in a jail shower, I have been walking in victory!
>
> A grateful recovering addict, Ben

What is one thing you can do today to help you move forward in the plan he has for you? Who can you call? What habit can you lay down? What strategies can you use at this moment to help you cope with your current emotion? Set that next goal or make the next step in your commitment to change. Where do you want to be in a year from now? Do the next best thing today to move forward and begin to experience life, liberty, and love!

# 36

# ALL'S NOT LOST
# WITH ALZHEIMER'S

*And I am certain that God, who began the good work within you,*
*will continue his work until it is finally finished on*
*the day when Christ Jesus returns.*
(Philippians 1:6)

A dreadful poem, attributed to the Alzheimer's Association, is being spread across social networks in which the author laments, "The best of me is gone."

Wrong! Wrong! Wrong! This couldn't be farther from the truth!

## Your best is in your children and grandchildren

If you are suffering from Alzheimer's, here's the good news. The best of you lives on in your children and grandchildren.* They carry your DNA and, in many ways, your personality. Your lifetime's influence, encouragement, and life lessons are not gone with your memories but live on in those you love.** The values and beliefs you modeled before your children and grandchildren also live on well beyond your years. The best of you is not gone!

## Your best is in your friends, co-workers, students, customers . . .

Unless you've spent your entire life alone on a deserted island, the best of you lives on in the lives of those you have offered help, taught a skill or life lesson, or provided a valuable service.

Your advice, admonitions, teaching, and mentoring will continue throughout their lives and the lives they influence. The best of you is not gone!

## Your best is in the lives your faith has touched

For followers of Jesus suffering from Alzheimer's, a lifetime of modeling your faith before family and friends has impacted the very Kingdom of God. If you have served as a Sunday school teacher, preacher, missionary, or faithful layperson, your best lives on in the eternally changed lives of those you served. The best of you is not gone!

## Your best is in you right now!

If you are farther down the path of Alzheimer's, you may not know today's date, recognize old friends, or even remember your spouse. He or she is simply a nice person who comes to see you each day. That nice person may be reading this chapter to you right now.

But even as your mind leaves this earth well before your body, it stands as a monument for what you stood for. It's a reminder of the love and influence you poured out on your family and friends. Think of yourself as a living photograph—it may be silent or even comatose—and yet it speaks love, faith, and courage.

R. J. Palacio writes, "The things we do are like monuments that people build to honor heroes after they've died. . . . Only instead of being made out of stone, they're made out of the memories people have of you."

Your good work is not finished! And the best of you is not gone!

## The best is yet to be

"On the day when Christ Jesus returns" you will be perfectly restored in mind and body. Jesus himself will greet you with the words "Well done, good and faithful servant." So even as you are dying to this world, eternal life awaits you. And in heaven, the dying memories of this world will be resurrected as you reunite with family and friends who have gone before you. The best of you is just beginning as you make the transition from earthly memories to eternal reality!

Adapted from *If You're Not Dead, You're Not Done!* by James N. Watkins

\* One of the greatest joys in my life is knowing Faith is a true follower of Christ and an amazing writer! I'd like to think I had a bit to do with that.

\*\* We all know that many individual traits are determined by genetics and our environment. But some scientists are theorizing a third influence: epigenetics. Genes are either expressed or suppressed in response to environmental and lifestyle factors, so "epigenetic marks" can be chemically transferred to the DNA of offspring across multiple generations. The research is still in the early stages.

## PRESCRIPTION

The anxiety associated with forgetting can be overwhelming, whether we have Alzheimer's or not. The following are some ways to be reminded of the important things in life, especially when it comes to being reminded of the lasting impact we have on others or remembering to pick up our children at school.

### ☐ Make a list or set a reminder

As a forty-plus person, I live and breathe by my Remind app. Any time something crosses my mind like a task or something I need at the store, I put it on the list. Even if you prefer a paper list, just remember to look at your list and remember where you put it. If it's an important event, I put it on my Google calendar as soon as it's scheduled. Thankfully a notification pops up when I need to remember it.

### ☐ Scrapbook

Scrapbooking is one of my favorite hobbies because it's a relaxing escape for me and fills my mind with happy memories. But more importantly, it's so entertaining to look through the scrapbooks with my girls, recalling memories and telling funny stories. Most importantly, these scrapbooks preserve our family memories for future generations. With my grandma's passing, I have been especially thankful for all the work that she put into preserving our family memories in old spiral-bound albums.

## ☐ Keep special cards and mementos

Over the years, I've received some very special encouragement cards from friends, family, and clients. I keep all of them in a plastic shoebox-sized tote that I've labeled "My Happy Box." This is something I've often pulled out when I need some encouragement or I forget that I am making a difference in the lives of people around me.

## ☐ Journal

Not only is journaling a helpful way to document events or express feelings and thoughts in the moment, but it also documents our journey of spiritual and emotional growth. Going back and reading them can be extremely embarrassing (please burn mine as soon as I die), but it can also be very helpful to remind you of what you have been through, how you have changed, and how far God has carried you. These are definitely things we want to remember.

## ☐ Talk to family or friends

I have the best time when we get together with family, especially when Grandma's old photo albums come out. It's amazing how one photo can spark so much reminiscing, storytelling, and laughing. I love asking questions and finding out more about life back in the Stone Age. Sharing memories with friends and family is a wonderful way to remember and recall the ups and downs of life and change our perspective.

## ☐ Consider your social or spiritual footprint

Watch *It's a Wonderful Life* for the first or fiftieth time, and you can't help but be reminded that we all make a difference in the lives of those around us, and we touch each one in a personal and powerful way that we may never see this side of heaven.

# X

# I AM ETERNAL

*In his kindness God called you to share in his eternal glory*
*by means of Christ Jesus. So after you have suffered*
*a little while, he will restore, support, and strengthen you,*
*and he will place you on a firm foundation.*

1 Peter 5:10

# 37

# "HI, I'M ELIJAH.
# I'M JUST REALLY TIRED!"

*"Come to me, all of you who are weary and carry heavy burdens,*
*and I will give you rest. Take my yoke upon you.*
*Let me teach you, because I am humble and gentle at heart,*
*and you will find rest for your souls. For my yoke is easy to bear,*
*and the burden I give you is light."*
Jesus, Matthew 11:28–30

An old man in a tattered robe raised his hand in the weekly Shalom Support Group. The group leader nodded to the renowned prophet.

"Hi, I'm Elijah, and I can certainly relate to those ups and downs we've been sharing about. It seems the higher the highs, the lower the lows that follow. For instance, you probably remember the big contest between me and the priests of Baal. I proposed that we set up an altar and see which of our gods could light it up.

"As you know, nothing happened for the pagan priests. In fact, as they were dancing and cutting themselves to get Baal's attention, I taunted them with, 'Maybe he's on the toilet. Shout louder'" (1 Kings 18:27). Ha!

"But as soon as I called out for Yahweh, our God sent a bolt of fire that evaporated the water I had poured on the altar for a bit of dramatic effect, consumed the wood and sacrificial bull—even melted the rocks of the altar. What a great display of God's power!"

Elijah suddenly bowed his head and stared at the floor. "But as soon as I heard that Queen Jezebel was also burned up about that, I ran an entire day's journey and collapsed under a broom tree. I told God, 'I have had enough, Lord. Take my life, for I am no better than my ancestors who have already died'" (1 Kings 9:4).

"God has been so good to me, but I'm just tired and ready to go to him. I've passed my prophetic powers onto a young up-and-comer named Elisha, and I expect him to experience two times the miracles God has done through me."

A knock on the door interrupted the prophet. "That must be the chariot I scheduled. My driver promises it's a hot ride!"

During a layover in New Zealand on our way to Australia, a man in a hazmat suit entered the plane with two cans of aerosol spray. With both hands wildly waving his cans, he marched down the aisle fumigating each passenger. We were told this was standard procedure to avoid our bringing in any plant diseases to the tropical paradise. That was memorable.

But so was the captain's warning to us as we caught our breaths and prepared to deplane. "Our time on the ground will be brief."

Now that I've just celebrated the big seven-zero birthday, that statement has taken on a new and deeper meeting. Our time on the ground *will be* brief.

I remember like it was yesterday being five years old and trying to sleep on Christmas Eve knowing that in the morning, there would be presents piled under the tree. Boom! That was sixty-five years ago.

It seems just a few years ago I was putting raisins in Kellogg's Raisin Bran between semesters at college. No smiling sun scooping raisins into the boxes. Nope! It was the dead of night as I was ripping open fifty-pound boxes of gobbed-together raisins and shoving them with a metal pole through a chute in the floor down to the packing room. I remember thinking that 6 AM would never, ever come. Boom! That was over fifty years ago.

I remember counting down the days before I returned home from a three-week teaching trip to India—the land without toilet paper! I thought the time would never pass. Boom! That was over twenty years ago.

Now I'm looking to the future and realizing that—Boom!—one day I'll be one hundred years old and life will have flown by. (My Aunt Millie lived to one hundred, and three of four grandparents lived into their late nineties, so I'm hoping to match them in longevity.) But even thirty years doesn't seem that long. That's frightening—and encouraging.

Yep, our time on the ground is brief! And so, I struggle like St. Paul:

> For to me, living means living for Christ, and dying is even better. But if I live, I can do more fruitful work for Christ. So I really don't know which is better. I'm torn between two desires: I long to go and be with Christ, which would be far better for me. But for your sakes, it is better that I continue to live (Philippians 1:21–24).

As great as trading in this old clunker of a body for a brand-new model seems, having a new mind is even more appealing! No more clinical depression. No more OCD. No more ADD. No more symptoms of ASD. No more uncomfortable introversion. And like the Scarecrow, I'm getting a brand-new brain!

* While Methuselah (Genesis 5:21-27) holds the all-time record of 969 candles on his birthday cake, the modern record for longest life is held by Jeanne Calment of France (1875–1997), who lived to age 122 years and 164 days. The oldest man was Jiroemon Kimura of Japan (1897–2013), who lived to age 116 years and 54 days.

### PRESCRIPTION

Handling layovers and life well, like Elijah, involves taking time to reflect on our past, make the most of our present moments, and look forward to our heavenly home.

☐ **Reflect**

On our layover, on the way home from Maui, we reminisced about all of the memories we made in the most beautiful place on this side of heaven.

What blessings have you experienced in your life, and how have you seen God move?

What have been the difficult seasons in your life? What are the lessons learned? How have you seen God work?

☐ **Look forward longingly**

Although Maui would not be in the budget for a very long time, we longed for the day we would be back.

What do you long for the most when you think about spending eternity with Jesus?

☐ **Make the most of the moment**

During that layover, we ate at a fun restaurant, shopped, and transferred all of our individual photos to our shared vacation album.

What are your current blessings? Praise God for the ways you are seeing him move even now.

What moments are making life hard right now? Share these with God or a trusted friend.

You can rest assured that our past and present sufferings of this "layover" won't last forever. You can look forward longingly knowing that your chariot ride for eternity is already booked, and will soon be boarding. We are going home!

# 38

# "CONVINCE ME NOT TO SHOOT MYSELF"

*How long must I struggle with anguish in my soul,*
*with sorrow in my heart every day? . . .*
*Turn and answer me, O Lord my God!*
*Restore the sparkle to my eyes, or I will die.*
Psalm 13:2–3

Several years ago, I wrote an article for Billy Graham's *Decision* magazine titled "Do Those Who Commit Suicide Go to Heaven?"* Short answer: Yes! Our salvation is based on our relationship with Jesus Christ—not on a mental health breakdown.

The only problem was the magazine, with a circulation in the millions, listed my home town of between three and four hundred people. So, it wasn't hard to go online and get my phone number.

One night, I answered the phone to hear, "Are you the guy that wrote that article about people that kill themselves can go to heaven?"

"Yes. How can I help you?"

"I'm sitting here with a loaded shotgun. Convince me not to shoot myself."

Thus, began nearly a month of frantic phone calls from desperate people contemplating suicide. Fortunately, all my callers were eventually talked off the ledge by my feeble and fumbling attempts. "Thank you, Father, Son, Spirit!"

## You are not alone

Globally, 800,000 people die from suicide every year. Twenty-five times that number attempt suicide annually. That is 1.4 percent of all deaths annually throughout the world. Compare that to COVID-19 deaths of 0.0008 percent. Let that sink in. Suicide is a pandemic 1,750 times more deadly than the virus! (Shouldn't that be the number one public health concern around the world? I see TV commercials every day for everything from eczema to E.D., but not one offering help for suicidal ideation.)

And yet, it is rarely talked about—especially in church. At the Shalom Support Group, we learned that Moses, Job, and Jeremiah all had serious suicidal ideations. But there were others.

After Jonah survived three days up to his chin in chum, and following a great revival in Nineveh, the prophet cried out, "Just kill me now, Lord! I'd rather be dead than alive" (4:3). And a bit later, "Death is certainly better than living like this!" (4.8).

King Saul died by assisted suicide (2 Samuel 1:6–10) and Judas hanged himself after betraying Jesus (Matthew 27:5).

My seven-year-old world was shaken as my second-grade teacher was telling about Jesus' love and the next week we learned she had hanged herself the night before. And I continue to grieve as I read of pastors of churches small and mega who have taken their own lives. One minister leading a program for those with depression shot himself.

So, please know that even in the Church, you are not alone. Hebrews 4:15 assures us that Jesus "understands our weaknesses, for he faced all of the same testings we do. . . ." I suspect—and it's pure speculation—Jesus thought, *I could kill myself and be spared prolonged torture and an excruciating death.*

## Hope and help are available

I used to drive by cemeteries and think *Lucky stiffs!* But when I started to scheme how to make my suicide look like an accident—I didn't want my family and friends to feel responsible—I knew I needed professional help.

If you are having thoughts of suicide, please put down this book right now and . . .

## Call or text 988

The new service which rolled out July 2022 will connect people to the existing network of more than two hundred local crisis call centers around the country. The National Suicide Prevention Lifeline's number will remain active, but calls will be routed to 988. If the service covering your area is busy, you will be automatically transferred to a professional in an adjoining area.

And speaking of professionals, I'm going to turn the rest of this chapter over to a professional: Faith, my daughter. It's great to have an expert in the family. (I just wish she had been living at home when those calls came in. "Faith, it's for you!")

## PRESCRIPTION

If you're having thoughts of suicide, and especially if you have a plan plus the means to accomplish it, follow Dad's advice and get help *now*.

Here are some other suggestions if you're not at that crisis point, but know you need professional help managing life and finding hope to continue living

☐ **See your family doctor as soon as possible**
Most family and general practice doctors are well-trained to start the process of mental healing and may put you on medication. Mental health services are covered by most insurances, but if you can't afford them, call your county health department. There are free services in every community.

Clients often have a lot of apprehension and fears about starting medications. However, research has shown over and over that the most effective treatment of mental health disorders is combining both medications and therapy.

In Chapter 32, Dad made a case for medication, even if you may feel like a lab rat as you work with your doctor to find the most effective one with the least side effects. Don't be discouraged or give up.

Dad's doctor prescribed five different antidepressants over time. They finally found just the right combination of two, and he has been depression-free for several years now. (Well, he does have severe depression just before he shares his story, but that's less serotonin and more satanic oppression.)

Also, starting medication now does not mean you are making a life-long commitment to taking pills until Jesus takes you home. We have various seasons in our lives that are more difficult than others, and we may need an extra mental and emotional boost. I know from personal experience that a small dose of medication can be totally life-changing.

## ☐ Talk to a trained professional

Meds are not a cure-all, so you will want to talk to a mental health professional as well. Your pastor, priest, or rabbi may be a great listener, but if he or she is not specifically trained to help with your need, call your local mental health center. (If you're well-known in your community, look for help in a nearby town.) And, again, if you feel you can't afford it, call your county health department. There are free mental health services available. Both Dad and I have greatly benefited from talking with a highly-trained Christian therapist.

## ☐ Prepare for your visit

I know there is much apprehension and fear about simply taking the first step to call for an appointment. Here's how to ease into it:

Most mental health agencies have websites with photos of therapists, along with their experiences, training, and specialties. This is a great way to check out the field before making that call or committing.

When you make the call, a receptionist will take your information, have you fill out paperwork, and will schedule the first appointment.

The first appointment will consist of the therapist getting to know you and your story, and asking a lot of questions. These will help the therapist get an overall picture of you as a person and your presenting problems and help create an effective treatment plan.

☐ **Make your needs known**

This is *your* treatment experience. If you don't feel like you click with the therapist, give it a couple more sessions, but be honest about your feelings. This is a sacred relationship, so if you don't feel comfortable or feel there is a disconnect, it's okay to ask about transferring to another therapist. Or, if you love your therapist, but feel there's a more pressing issue that needs to be addressed, please let them know. As a therapist, I always want to know if what we are doing isn't working and need to try another approach. This is your life and your story, so advocate for yourself.

And remember . . .

☐ **If you need immediate help, please call or text 988**.

# 39

# A WEEK-LONG WEDDING FEAST

*Let us be glad and rejoice, and let us give honor to him.*
*For the time has come for the wedding feast of the Lamb.*
Revelation 19:7

When the resurrected Jesus first appeared to his disciples, one of the first things he said was, "Do you have anything here to eat?" (I love it! That was always the first question I asked when I came home from college.) "They gave him a piece of broiled fish, and he ate it as they watched" (Luke 24:41–43).

At his third appearance to his disciples, Jesus had "breakfast waiting for them—fish cooking over a charcoal fire, and some bread" (John 21:9).

Finally, when we are resurrected in heaven with Christ, we will sit down for a wedding feast. This will be no reception with finger food and a slice of cake! Nope. A Jewish wedding feast—called *simcha* or "joyous occasion"—lasted at least a week!*

But wait, there's more! Heaven features its own version of the "Fruit of the Month" club: "On each side of the river grew a tree of life, bearing twelve kinds of fruit, with a fresh crop each month" (Revelation 22:2).

So, what's my point? Simple: Our resurrected bodies will enjoy food and drink, without any of the earthly side effects like anorexia, bulimia, or any other eating disorders! And apparently, no obesity, high cholesterol, or acid reflux! I'm also assuming there will be no body dysphoria since we're all wearing flowing robes. That is indeed good news for the thirty-million Americans who suffer from some form of an eating disorder.

Whether it's restricting intake or binging/purging, the National Institute of Health warns people with eating disorders have an extremely high death rate compared to other disorders. And suicide is the second leading cause of death for those with eating disorders.

An NIH reports eating disorders can lead to . . .

> . . . thinning of the bones (osteopenia or osteoporosis); mild anemia, muscle wasting, and weakness; severe constipation; low blood pressure; slowed breathing and pulse; damage to the structure and function of the heart; brain damage; organ failure; drop in internal body temperature, causing a person to feel cold all the time; lethargy, sluggishness, or feeling tired all the time; [and] infertility.

If you're dealing with an eating disorder, know that help is available through your family doctor or a professional therapist.

And also know, that heaven will offer joyous freedom from any mental or physical health issue! Even healing from any "insults and mockery" you've endured.

> He will swallow up death forever! The Sovereign Lord will wipe away all tears. He will remove forever all insults and mockery. . . . The Lord has spoken! (Isaiah 25:8).

And Jesus promises:

> "There is more than enough room in my Father's home. If this were not so, would I have told you that I am going to prepare a place for you? When everything is ready, I will come and get you, so that you will always be with me where I am" (John 14:2–3).

I am so looking forward to my new body and new mind! But not too much or that would be a whole 'nother mental health issue. But in comparison to eternity, the time I will have lived on this fallen world with my failing mind will be infinitely infinitesimal!

\* An important part of the ancient Hebrew wedding celebration was the *yichud* meaning "together." The groom would carry his bride off to the house he had prepared for them where they would get to "know" each other. (Wink. Wink.) The two would then return to the cheers of the wedding party.

## PRESCRIPTION

My friend, Summer, now 40-something, began struggling with anorexia in her junior year of high school. She admitted to me, "It has always been difficult for me to talk about that part of my journey, but I really feel like for some reason this is the season that God wants me to share my story." This is Summer's story along with the insights she has learned along the way.

☐ **Learn and understand as much as you can about the nature of disordered eating**

Know that it is *very* rare for an eating disorder to be about eating or even food. Having a sense of control is at the very core of an eating disorder. Similarly, eating disorders are a very serious form of addiction. Someone with an eating disorder has very similar beliefs, thoughts, emotions, urges, and behavior patterns to someone addicted to drugs, except that food is everywhere they turn. Just like it's not just that easy to quit using drugs, it's not a simple matter of just eating more.

As a missionary kid growing up in another country, attending a boarding school for English kids away from my parents, as well as the general angst of adolescence, the choice to eat or not to eat was the one thing in my life that I could control. I eventually got to the point of needing to throw up after every meal, like an automatic instinct. Honestly, I thought I would never be free of it.

☐ **Be mindful of how our language may be subtly teaching or reinforcing for others**

A simple compliment to someone who has lost weight is typically positive, motivating, and welcomed. But the same compliment for someone with an eating disorder can reinforce their addictive eating disorder cycle. Their brain is automatically wired to think, "Hmm? When I binge and purge or restrict food, people think I am beautiful. Therefore, if I am to be beautiful and accepted, I must binge/purge or restrict food."

I remember having negative thoughts about my body beginning in late elementary when my extended family began commenting that I was putting on weight. Those messages and well-meaning comments were deeply implanted in my heart and mind as I grew and developed. As I began to lose more and more weight people began commenting on how great I looked. It made me feel beautiful and seen.

Consider these questions: When I am around others, do I criticize myself, my body, or my weight? Am I dieting all the time in an endless cycle? Do I make comments about the weight of others?

☐ **Be conscious of the "Food as Fuel" fallacy**

If not a life-threatening inpatient situation, trying to fight or argue with a person with disordered eating about food being fuel for their body can honestly fall on deaf ears. Pushing food as the fuel for one's body when he or she is actively involved in an eating disorder makes it more food-focused, and we have learned that it is not all about the food. Food is not the only form of fuel for a body. Encouragement, prayers, time spent with them, believing them, and listening to them are also forms of fuel. We want to want to fuel the heart, mind, soul, *and* body.

☐ **There is help available for the one suffering from an eating disorder and support for their loved ones**

If you find that you meet the criteria of addiction from Chapter 35 as it relates to food, eating, and/or body image, know that there is help available. The most successful treatment includes a team of providers including a physician, a nutritionist, and mental health professional. Summer shared two exercises that her therapist had her do.

Any time you sit down to a meal, picture Jesus either across from you. What would he want you to feel or know about yourself and your body? What would he say about food? About your body? About your soul and your worth? Let Jesus' voice be louder than the lies being shouted at you.

☐ **Understand your eternal value and worth, and how he will redeem your story for his eternal glory**

God takes the broken and shattered pieces of our lives and gives us restoration and healing in its place. Whether you struggle with a negative body image, * disordered eating, or a clinically diagnosed eating disorder, ask God to give you the strength and courage to overcome and to know your eternal worth and value.

> Twenty years after surrendering my eating disorder into his hands, God has started bringing young girls into my life who are struggling like I was and giving me the opportunity to mentor and disciple them, showing them the road to freedom. I am reminded more and more of how God uses the healing we have received to bring healing to others for their good, and his eternal glory.

Both Summer and I look forward to that glorious day, when we will sit down at the wedding feast with Jesus, completely free from the bondage to this earthly body with its addictions, eating disorders, depression, anxieties, traumas, etc. We will be able to truly eat, drink, and be merry!

** A great resource is *Breaking Free from Body Shame: Dare to Reclaim What God Has Named* by Jess Connolly (Zondervan 2021).

# 40

# IT'S ONLY TEMPORARY

*The suffering won't last forever. It won't be long*
*before this generous God . . . will have you put together*
*and on your feet for good.*
1 Peter 5:10 MSG

D
o you ever feel like Humpty Dumpty, the egghead from the nursery rhyme?* Mental illness has pushed you off the wall, and there you lie: broken with your insides oozing out for all the world to see. That shell of "normalcy" has been cracked wide open and you feel exposed, humiliated, and helpless. And all the king's horses and all the king's men— along with all the doctors and therapists—haven't been able to put you together again.

Whatever mental health challenge you are facing from anxiety to zoophobia (fear of animals), you may feel hopeless. You've been to every specialist and have tried every psychotropic drug currently FDA-approved, and you are still lying broken and exposed on the ground. You may even be reading this in the closed section of a mental hospital. (Christians including singer Sheila Walsh and comedian Chonda Pierce having openly admitted their time behind locked doors.)

But I want to assure you—as awful as it actually is—it's only temporary. There is hope. Eugene Peterson paraphrased 1 Peter 5:9b–11 this way:

> You're not the only ones plunged into these hard times.
> It's the same with Christians all over the world. So keep
> a firm grip on the faith. The suffering won't last forever.

It won't be long before this generous God who has great plans for us in Christ—eternal and glorious plans they are!—will have you put together and on your feet for good. He gets the last word; yes, he does (MSG).

First Peter was written in or around AD 63 to a group of Christians living in modern-day Turkey, just south of the Black Sea. Isolated persecution of Christians had broken out during this time, but this group of believers was not suffering any formal or life-threatening persecution.

But according to 1 Peter 3:16 in various translations, they were being "falsely accused," "insulted," "maligned," "slandered," and "spoken evil of."

Ever felt that way about being a Christian? And being a Christian with mental health issues, you're treated even worse by both the church and the world! Remember these key points quoted from 1 Peter 5 earlier:

**I'm not the only one plunged into these hard times.**

**My suffering won't last forever.**

**It won't be long before this generous God . . . will have me put together and on my feet for good.**

I believe we can claim these promises for our mental health as well. Our "generous God" will restore us to perfect physical and mental health. He will put us together and on our feet for good—for eternity. Remember, it's only temporary!

* Several theories surround the origin of the famous egg who fell off a wall. Many believe Humpty Dumpty is King Richard III of England, who is supposed to have been humpbacked and who was defeated at the Battle of Bosworth Field in 1485. He fell from his throne and "all the king's horses and all the king's men" couldn't restore him to power.

## PRESCRIPTION

Up until recently, I thought I had seen the full extent of human suffering and pain over the seventeen years I've been in practice. After all, I've met with mothers and fathers who have lost their children to suicide or overdose. I have sat with people who have experienced physical and sexual abuse beyond anyone's wildest nightmares. And I have seen lives and families torn apart by the insane grip of addiction on one's life. I thought I had seen it all, that was until Ruth walked into my office a few months ago.

As a child, Ruth was the victim of horrific and unspeakable acts done to her in the name and worship of pure evil. Just last week, she had the most intense flashback I have ever witnessed, in which she curled up on my couch in the fetal position begging "them" to stop hurting her. My heart literally felt like it was breaking, and I watched her being tormented by her own memories and did my best to bring her back to reality in my office where she was safe.

Because of this chronic early childhood trauma, she developed Dissociative Identity Disorder (DID) previously referred to as Multiple Personality or Split Personality. DID is very rare and often the result of sexual or physical abuse during childhood. Ruth became so overwhelmed by the ritualistic trauma that her brain developed this disorder as a way to distance or detach herself from the immense pain and suffering she was experiencing.

But unfortunately, her development of DID and the influence of the demonic forces that were introduced to her early on have done nothing to alleviate the immense suffering and have actually led to more affliction. Ruth is the core personality, but she has at least twenty-five "alters" or alternate personalities. These alters come in and out of our sessions like a revolving door, leaving my head spinning all while trying to keep track of who exactly came to the session that day. Some alters are willing participants in treatment and others hate me and the healing that I represent. Ruth has accepted Christ and is a Christ-follower and Jesus-lover at her core, along with other alters who do not believe. Both the believing and unbelieving alters have begged and pleaded with me to help them. Through tears, they have cried out, "You have to help me. Please help me" or "Can you help us? Can you help Ruth?"

In her suffering and anguish, she asks tough questions like, "Why won't God take this from me? Why am I suffering like this? Does he even love me or care?" At those questions, all of my therapeutic techniques and theories go out the window. All my heart desperately wants is for her to know the truth about her innate value and worth, despite her trauma and a diagnosis of DID.

Here are some strategies to help us shift our thinking to an eternal, hope-filled perspective, no matter what issue you are facing:

☐ **Write down in your journal what suffering and pain you are experiencing in this fallen world.**

☐ **Imagine, then list, ways your mind and body will be made new in eternity**

☐ **Remind yourself of this hope when you are overwhelmed by suffering in the present**

Although we don't know the day or hour, we do know that we will have a brand-new body free of the limitations and heartache of this life.

Meanwhile, we can do our best to make the most of the time we have in this broken world by loving others, loving ourselves, taking care of our physical and/or mental health, and loving God with all of our heart, soul, mind, body, and strength. Even now, where you sit, he is in the process of restoring you and making you new.

Someday, on the other side of eternity, I'll bump into Ruth—and I won't even recognize her. The grimace on her face brought on by a life of torment by alters and demonic forces will glow with the glory and healing of Jesus. She won't be confined to shuffling along with a walker because of the vicious toll that unspeakable abuse and mental illness have taken on her body over the years. She will have a new body and a new mind, fully aware of who she is as a daughter of the King, and free to worship her Savior for eternity. I literally get giddy inside thinking about the glorious freedom she will experience from this horrific life she has lived here on earth.

And although I'm not physically there with you, and I don't know you or what suffering you have faced in this life, I can't wait to bump into you on those streets of gold in heaven. I want to sit by the crystal sea and hear the story of how you have been made completely, thoroughly, and radically new, free from the pain and suffering of this life. The pain and suffering are only temporary! Until we finally make it to our eternal home and meet in person, let's praise the Lord and pass the Prozac.

# COMMENCEMENT AT THE SHALOM SUPPORT GROUP

*In my distress I cried out to the Lord;*
*yes, I prayed to my God for help. He heard me from*
*his sanctuary; my cry to him reached his ears.*
Psalm 18:6

Jacob rose to his feet and looked around the circle of now dear friends. "Before we begin today's meeting, have any of you seen Elijah since our last meeting? I heard he just took off.

"Well, this is a very special meeting of our Shalom Support Group." He self-consciously wiped his eye. We want to welcome each of you as we celebrate those who have applied every one of the Ten Affirmations. Well, *completed* is not really the right word. I hope you will carry this message and encouragement to the still suffering, and practice these principles in all your affairs.*

I've asked King David to share a few words as he receives his bronze coin for embracing our affirmations this last year. Your highness, the floor is yours."

The group cheered and applauded wildly as the king approached the lectern.

"Please, please. Be seated. In the Shalom Support Group, we are all on the same level as beloved children of the Most High God. Affirmation Number IV, correct?"

Jacob nodded yes.

"I'd just like to share a few things I've learned. I think the overall principles of this Big Book are . . .

## You are valuable in the eyes of your Creator

"We are loved. We are seen. We are important." Moved by the truth of this statement, Photine wrapped her arm around Hagar's shoulder and pulled her close.

"In God's eyes, you are just as valuable as your king, and his men as the man who scoops up donkey dung from our streets.

"Which brings me to Gideon. You may not feel like you're important, but you are an important member of this group and to the people of Israel. In fact, I would like to appoint you as my Chairman of the Joint Chiefs of Staff." And I'm sure you can keep our costs down with your unique strategy and weaponry.** The spontaneous chant of "Migh-ty warrior!" once again broke out in the group, as Gideon pulled his hood over his face. "I'd be honored, your majesty."

"And a special shout out to Lee of Gerasene. This man's got the strength of a thousand men, which is why I work out at his new health and fitness center: "God's Bods." But again, every one of us is equally valued in Jehovah's eyes. There is no one greater, no one less."

"And the second thing that has impressed me as we have gone through this study is . . . "

COMMENCEMENT AT THE SHALOM SUPPORT GROUP

## You are valuable in the eyes of your family, friends, and community

"Martha, you always make the most delicious snacks for our group meetings and come early to make sure that everything is perfect for everyone when they arrive. You make us all feel special with your attention to every little detail. It's a good thing!

"And Rahab, you are so faithful to unlock the room, spread out the mats, and welcome newcomers and long-time members to the group with open arms each week. You have such a gift of hospitality. In fact, every single one of you here is so important to me and to each other."

"Of course," Peter shouted from the back of the room. "We're important because we all pay taxes!"

Jacob rolled his eyes. "My apologies, your highness. He's always saying something inappropriate."

The king smiled. "Peter, our uptight society needs you with your outspoken nature, rough social skills, and passion for the Messiah. I love it . . . but do expect to be audited."

Peter's eyes widened, and his face turned pale.

"Ha! Just kidding, my friend. We're good."

"While working the Ten Affirmations, I have learned that my mental health issues with depression and mania are ways I can praise Jehovah through writing down the emotions of my ups and downs of my spiritual life. Who knows, maybe they will be helpful to future generations. So, as our resident therapist, Faith, has encouraged us to do, keep journaling. And we wouldn't have such depth of spiritual writing without our own weeping prophet, Jeremiah. Thanks, brother. Jehovah is able to work through our weaknesses with his amazing power.

"Those are what I think are the most important things to remember: One, you are valuable in the eyes of your Creator. And two, you are valuable in the eyes of your family, friends, and community. But I guess that would make a very short course, wouldn't it? And our group's scribe, James, would have very little to do.

"So, maybe one thing more thing . . ."

## We are valuable to each other with our encouragement and accountability

"That is what is so important about a support group like this. Because someone needs to stand up and tell you when you have so miserably messed up. So, thanks, Nathan. And I so needed all of your encouragement when my child with Bathsheba died soon after birth, and I need all of your prayers and support as my family members keep making the evening news with some new scandal. Oy vey, my family puts the "dys" in dysfunction!

"Let me close with one of my favorite psalms. I wrote this right after the Lord saved me from the wrath of King Saul. That guy had serious mood swings!

> "I love you, Lord;
> you are my strength.
> The Lord is my rock, my fortress, and my savior;
> my God is my rock, in whom I find protection.
> He is my shield, the power that saves me,
> and my place of safety.
> I called on the Lord, who is worthy of praise,
> and he saved me from my enemies.
>
> "But in my distress, I cried out to the Lord;
> yes, I prayed to my God for help.
> He heard me from his sanctuary;
> my cry to him reached his ears" (Psalm 18:1–3, 6).

"So, 'be strong and courageous, and do the work. Don't be afraid or discouraged, for the Lord God, my God, is with you. He will not fail you or forsake you'" (1 Chronicles 28:20).

All stood and embraced one another. "Praise be to our God and Savior!"

* This is the final phrase in the twelfth step of recovery. We pray that you find hope and help as you "practice these principles in all your affairs."

** Learn how Gideon defeated one-hundred-thousand men with just three hundred men armed with clay pitchers, torches, and trumpets (What?!) in Judges 7.

## PRESCRIPTION

Although you may not have David's same story, chances are you picked up this book because you were at a point in your life of feeling broken, beaten down, and overwhelmed by your mental health or your difficult life circumstances.

Like David, you may have been in a place of hopelessness and desperation, but God found you, and you have heard him speak to you through this book. God has a way of finding us in our moments of distress and despair with the true and lasting hope and healing he has to offer. Our hope and prayer are that God has met you here on these pages and you have heard his gentle voice and experienced the same stirring in your heart that David did in those dark places.

I am praying for you as I write this that you will allow him to transform you and give you an ongoing desire to create a life worth living with his help and power.

☐ **Surrender to the higher power**
Just as with David, starting on the journey of spiritual recovery and renewal is as easy as A-B-C: Admit, Believe, Commit. If you haven't already surrendered your life to Jesus, I want to give you the opportunity here and now. You can pray this simple prayer out loud or in your heart:

> God, I am broken and battered by this life, my mental health, my trauma, and my own choices. I know I can't keep going on like this anymore. I have come to believe that you are the only one who can help me and restore me. You created the world and everything in it, and still, you see me and know me in my heartaches and brokenness.

You have been pursuing me and calling me to you and your heart. If that isn't enough, you sent your own son to die on the cross to ransom me and my heart so that I can be yours and live with you forever. I can never fully thank you for all you've done, but I offer myself and my life as an offering of praise and thanks back to you. No matter what life brings, I am yours. Amen.

If you prayed this prayer, I am beyond excited for you. Sincerely admitting your weaknesses, believing that he died and came back for you, and committing your life to him will radically change you. I promise.

## ☐ Tell someone about your decision

Your next step is to tell someone—a friend, a pastor, a family member—anyone who can help you take the next steps in your faith journey. Remember all the way back to the beginning chapter: You are not alone!

## ☐ Come back to him

Maybe you've prayed this prayer before, perhaps years ago, but life has battered you and your faith has shattered. You started to question everything you knew about God and turned away from him. If, by reading this book, you have come to a place where you want to recommit yourself to the ultimate source of healing, please go back and pray this prayer out loud or in your heart. Come back to him and recommit your all to him even the ugly, messed up parts of you. If you did pray this prayer, I will say the same for you as I did to the brand-new believer: Tell someone who can help you take the next steps in your faith journey. You are not alone!

## ☐ Hold on tight!

Perhaps you have been a Jesus follower for months or years and your faith is the only thing that has kept you going, hiding in the shelter of his wings or clinging for dear life to the rock of your salvation. Over the years, the waves of life have crashed over me, slamming me up against the rocks, leaving me broken and battered. In the process, I lost myself and my faith was shaken. The pages of this book are filled with stories of others who have been pounded and thrashed around by the storms of life. Dad has honestly and transparently shared his own struggles throughout the stormy seas of life. Know that God is with you in the storm. Keep holding tight, you are not alone!

## ☐ Stay Open

Even if you are still questioning this whole faith thing, struggling to believe these 10 affirmations or trusting the God who speaks them over you, please stay open to him even if you aren't ready to make a commitment here and now. You picked up this book for a reason, and I trust that if nothing else, God has been giving you glimpses of his unfailing love and faithfulness through these pages. Maybe it's hard for you to see it through the hurt, pain, or even trauma that the church, religion, or others have caused you, but just know that the God of the universe loves you more than any other human ever could. He is patient and will keep waiting for you to come to him, all the while pursuing you with his love. Just be open to it.

So "What's next?" you ask. It's time to commit to doing the next best thing and setting some continued goals that will help you keep making changes, long after you have finished this book. Healing is a lifelong process until we are completely and totally restored when we enter eternity with him.

## ☐ Keep on the journey of RECOVERY

For now, let's take a look at the different areas of our lives and start creating a plan for continued life, liberty, and love. The best way to ensure that a commitment is followed is, you guessed it, writing it down in black and white in your journal. Once you've written it down, share it with a close friend, accountability partner, or therapist. The real journey of RECOVERY starts now!

**R-eflect.** David spent a lot of time in the Psalms reflecting on the journey of his people, the Israelites, and his own personal narrative. This helped him get a clear picture of who he used to be, who he was now, and who God is to him.

Ask yourself these questions and then journal your responses:

> What state was I in emotionally, physically, relationally, and spiritually when I started reading this book? Be specific.
>
> In what ways have I grown or changed in these areas over the last forty chapters? Write down some specific examples.
>
> Moving forward, these are three specific goals I would like to achieve in the next three months:

**E-motional Health.** During his times of darkness, David cried out to God and was honest with him and with himself about his difficult beliefs, thoughts, emotions, behaviors, and the difficult outcomes of his own reactions and the actions of others.

> What unhealthy or untrue beliefs or thoughts do I need to change?
>
> What specific steps do I need to take for my mental and emotional wellbeing?
>
> Do I need to make an appointment with a therapist, a doctor, or join a support group? If so, I will do it by this date:

**C-oping Skills.** David gives us hundreds of examples of ways he coped with difficult feelings, even when his circumstances didn't change.

> What specific prescriptions in this book have I tried, and I have begun to feel some healing?
>
> What are specific prescriptions that I haven't tried, but that I think might be helpful?

Moving forward, I will make a commitment to practice these prescriptions or coping skills consistently by:

**O-ther People.** David surrounded himself with people who were wise
and offered him feedback about his life, even when it meant confronting
him harshly. David grew more and more into "the man after God's own
heart" through this accountability from others and living in community.

Who are the people in my life who have negatively
contributed to my mental health? What are effective ways
to minimize their influence?

Who are the people in my life who are encouraging,
life-giving, hold me accountable, and want the best for
me? List specific names.

What are the specific steps I will take to surround
myself with these positive people? Get out your calendar
and start scheduling coffee dates or lunch dates.

**V-itality.** David took care of his physical body as well. He had the
strength and physical power to kill Goliath and cut his head off, kill
bears and lions, and conquer nations in battle. Clearly, his workouts at
God's Bods were paying off. He also knew when to let his body rest in
green meadows beside peaceful streams.

What are some of the health problems I am experiencing as a result of my mental health or in general?

What are some specific steps I can take to better care
of the body and mind God has blessed me with?

In what ways can I slow down my pace and find the
rest my body and soul need?

**E-ternal Mindset.** David knew that the life he was living was not
the end-game. He relied on his relationship with God to sustain him

during some of the most desperate, rock bottom moments in his life. He meditated on Scripture and spent great amounts of time praying to and worshiping God.

What has God taught me about who he is and his spiritual truths throughout these forty chapters?

What have I learned about myself, my faith, and my relationship with him?

What specific steps do I need to take to nurture my spirituality and my relationship with God? I will take one step today by . . .

**R-easons.** David had a lot of motivation for following his RECOVERY plan. He had been promised that the Messiah would come to rule through his family line. He lived life with purpose and to honor the covenant he made with God. He wanted to leave a legacy that would ultimately bring glory to the King of Kings.

What were the reasons I chose to purchase this book? What was I believing, thinking, or feeling at the time?

What are my reasons for continuing on this healing journey even after reading the last sentence of this book?

Who else will benefit from me reading this book and making the changes I have already made and will continue to make?

**Y-ou are not alone.** You are loved, seen, important, planned, forgiven, present, empowered, victorious, and eternal.

David knew these truths, however, through his year-long pursuit of healing in the Shalom

Support Group, he began to fully embrace and walk in these truths each day.

What from this book were the top three spiritual affirmations that made the most impact on me, my identity,
and my mental health?

Write a letter to God thanking him for these ten truths
and the things he has taught you as you read this book.

What specific actions can I take to continue to walk in
these truths each day of my life?

In what ways can I spread the life-changing message
of these spiritual affirmations to others in my life who
may still be hurting? Be specific.

As David came to the end of his reign and blessed his son Solomon
who would inherit his throne, he shared these final words:

"So now, with God as our witness, and in the sight of
all Israel—the Lord's assembly—I give you this charge.
Be careful to obey all the commands of the Lord your
God, so that you may continue to possess this good land
and leave it to your children as a permanent inheritance.
And [your name], my child, learn to know the God of your
ancestors intimately. Worship and serve him with your
whole heart and a willing mind. For the Lord sees every
heart and knows every plan and thought. If you seek him,
you will find him. But if you forsake him, he will reject
you forever. So take this seriously. The Lord has chosen
you to [fill in the blank with what you sense he is calling
to do]. Be strong, and do the work." (Chronicles 28:8–9).

Even thousands of years later, Dad and I echo these same truths that
David came to learn throughout his struggle with mental illness, trauma,
and poor decisions:

**You are not alone**

I am here with you, and Jesus is here in this room with you, too.

**You are loved**

. . . by the creator of the universe, and you are his precious child.

**You are seen**

. . . right now at this moment—even as you are suffering.

**You are important**

. . . and treasured in his eyes. I don't know the purpose of your pain and suffering, but I *do* know that . . .

**You are planned**

. . . and your Creator is writing a story of healing and redemption even now. You are covered in Jesus' blood and . . .

**You are forgiven**

. . . despite what the enemy tells you.

**You are present**

. . . in the here and now and you are safe with Him.

**You are empowered**

. . . with the holy spirit and . . .

**You are victorious**

. . . in Christ, and you will be victorious over your demons because . . .

**You are eternal**

. . . right now! And in Christ, you will have an eternal home with him filled with his love, joy, and peace.

# KEEP IN TOUCH

**Keep in touch with James**

    Email: jim@jameswatkins.com

    Facebook: @jameswatkinsauthor

    Instagram: @jameswatkinsauthor

    Web: jameswatkins.com

**Keep in touch with Faith**

    Email: faithawatkins@yahoo.com

    Facebook: Recovering Love: Faith A. Watkins

    Instagram: @faith.watkins.writer

    Web: RecoveringLove.com

# RESOURCES

Here are some additional resources that we hope are helpful. (These are live links at jameswatkins.com/prozac.)

The American Association of Christian Counselors
www.aacc.net/

American Psychological Association
www.apa.org/

American Psychiatric Association
www.psychiatry.org/

Anxiety and Depression Association of America
https://adaa.org/

Autism Speaks
www.autismspeaks.org/

Celebrate Recovery
www.celebraterecovery.com

DivorceCare
www.divorvecare.org

Focus on the Family
www.focusonthefamily.com/get-help/mental-health-resources/

Grief Share
www.griefshare.org

Healthline
www.healthline.com/health/mental-health-resources

National Alliance of Mental Illness
www.nami.org/Home

National Eating Disorder Association
www.nationaleatingdisorders.org/

National Institute of Mental Health
www.nimh.nih.gov

National Institute on Aging
www.nia.nih.gov/health

National Suicide Prevention Lifeline
suicidepreventionlifeline.org/
Call 998

Psychology Today
www.psychologytoday.com

United States Substance Abuse and Mental Health Service Administration
www.samhsa.gov

United States Department of Veteran's Affairs
www.mentalhealth.va.gov/

# BOOKS AND BLOGS
# BY THE WATKINS

*God, I Don't Understand: Struggling with Unanswered Prayer,*
*Unfulfilled Promises, Unpunished Evil*
James N. Watkins
Bold Vision Books

*If You're Not Dead, You're Not Done!*
James N. Watkins
Tyndale House Publishers

*The Imitation of Christ: Classic Devotions in Today's Language*
James N. Watkins
Worthy Inspired

*Intimacy with Christ*
James N. Watkins
CLC Publishers

*Overcoming Fear and Worry*
James N. Watkins
Our Daily Bread Publishers

*Squeezing Good Out of Bad*
James N. Watkins
Hope&Humor Books

*Jesus: His Life and Lessons*
James N. Watkins
Hope&Humor Books

Coming soon!
*Recovering Love*
Faith A. Watkins
recoveringlove.com

# ACKNOWLEDGMENTS

Thanks to Saint Lois of LaValle for remaining married to me (Jim) for nearly fifty years. Lots of love and gratitude for your faithful support of me and my crazy ideas! Great is your reward in heaven!

Thanks to my co-author. daughter, and great friend, Faith Anne LCSW, whose professional expertise has made the book so very personal and professional. Let's do this again!

Thanks as well to my fourteen-year-old grandson and amazing artist, Nathan Watkins, who brought our affirmations to life with his anthropomorphic pill bottles. We are honored to be your first paying clients!

Thanks to Tiffany Senabandith for her beautiful song to serve as the "prelude" to our book. Praying it goes viral!

Thanks to editor Jeanette Littleton and designer Robin Black for their patience and grace in working with an author who is a Type-A control freak with OCD: The trifecta of a challenging client. It was a joy to work with you both! I owe you each a Costco-size bottle of Tylenol and antiacids.

Thanks to Lissa Halls Johnson, Jeanette Levellie, and Cec Murphey for all the free therapy. You've always let me share my quirks and questions without criticism or condemnation—just compassion and prayer! You are faithful friends.

Finally, thanks to my Facebook "focus group," which provided valuable feedback on content and design as well as encouragement to keep working on this project.

**James Watkins**

To my girls, Hannah and Kaylah, I know it has been a sacrifice for all of us as I've been working on this project with Papaw. I am thankful for your understanding, encouragement, and love through this process. You have always been my two greatest motivations and reasons to heal, grow, and be the best version of myself. You have always kept me going even when I felt like giving up, and I love you more than you will ever comprehend.

Also, to my friends, Suzanne and LaSonda, for being my constant friends over the years through all of the good, the bad, and the ugly. Your friendship, accountability, encouragement, and unconditional love have kept me going on days when I felt completely overwhelmed with the battles of life. We've laughed, cried, and even sat in silence together when there were just no words. I couldn't ask for better friends, soul sisters, and personal "therapists" to navigate this crazy life with.

And to my Dad and co-author, for giving me the honor and privilege of walking this journey with you, trusting me in the process, and giving me a way to give honor and glory to God with the gifts and abilities he has blessed me with. I wouldn't want to make my writing debut with anyone else. You are the best co-author, dad, and friend that a girl could ask for.

Finally, to my brave clients who show up week after week in my office to face their traumatic pasts, overwhelming presents, and uncertain futures. It is an honor to walk alongside you through this leg of your life's journey and to help you discover healing and freedom. Your strength, determination, and courage inspire me every day, and I am in awe of you. Keep fighting the good fight!

**Faith Watkins**

I AM NOT ALONE
I AM LOVED
I AM SEEN
I AM IMPORTANT
I AM PLANNED
I AM FORGIVEN
I AM PRESENT
I AM EMPOWERED
I AM VICTORIOUS
I AM ETERNAL

PRAISE THE LORD AND PASS THE PROZAC
JAMESWATKINS.COM/PROZAC

www.ingramcontent.com/pod-product-compliance
Lightning Source LLC
Chambersburg PA
CBHW051818090426

42736CB00011B/1541